D0953709

The Greatest of Friends

Franklin D. Roosevelt and Winston Churchill
1941–1945

The Greatest of Friends

*Franklin D. Roosevelt
and Winston Churchill
1941–1945*

KEITH ALLDRITT

St. Martin's Press ❧ New York

© Keith Alldritt 1995
First published in Great Britain 1995

ISBN 0 7090 5266 9

Robert Hale Limited
Clerkenwell House
Clerkenwell Green
London EC1R 0HT

2   4   6   8   10   9   7   5   3   1

THE GREATEST OF FRIENDS: FRANKLIN D. ROOSEVELT AND WINSTON CHURCHILL, 1941-1945. Copyright
© 1995 by Keith Alldritt. All rights reserved. Printed in the United States of America. No
part of this book may be used or reproduced in any manner whatsoever without written
permission except in the case of brief quotations embodied in critical articles or reviews. For
information, address St. Martin's Press, 175 Fifth Avenue, New York, N.Y. 10010.

Library of Congress Cataloging-in-Publication Data

Alldritt, Keith.
    The greatest of friends : Franklin D. Roosevelt and Winston
Churchill, 1941-1945 / Keith Alldritt.
        p.   cm.
    ISBN 0-312-13505-X
    1. Roosevelt, Franklin D. (Franklin Delano), 1882-1945.
2. Churchill, Winston, Sir, 1874-1965.   3. World War, 1939-1945—
Diplomatic history.   4. United States—Foreign relations—Great
Britain.   5. Great Britain—Foreign relations—United States.
I. Title.
D748.A45   1995
940.53'2241—dc20   95-36361
                                                    CIP

First published in Great Britain by Robert Hale Limited

First U.S. Edition: December 1995
10 9 8 7 6 5 4 3 2 1

Contents

List of Illustrations   9
Acknoweldgements   11
Introduction   13
Prelude   17

 1   A Pen Friendship   37
 2   Getting to Know You   51
 3   Together at Christmas   75
 4   A Friend in Need   85
 5   Counsels and Contemplations   99
 6   Reassurances and Recitations   123
 7   Being Made at Home   139
 8   Two's Company but ...   153
 9   Jealousy   167
10   In the Time of Overlord   181
11   Coda   197

Select Bibliography   217
Index   221

FOR JOAN
AS ALWAYS
WITH LOVE

Illustrations

1 Roosevelt supported by his son Elliott is welcomed aboard HMS *Prince of Wales* by Churchill
2 Roosevelt and Churchill on *Prince of Wales* in Placentia Bay, Newfoundland
3 In a relaxed mood together after the service
4 Churchill watching the destroyer USS *McDougal* leaving Placentia Bay
5 Churchill in the gardens of the White House with Harry Hopkins, Deana Hopkins and Commander Thompson
6 Roosevelt drives Churchill, Brendan Bracken and Commander Thompson in his specially equipped car
7 Resting in the rose garden after long discussions in the White House
8 A confidential moment at Casablanca
9 Endeavouring to maintain straight faces with de Gaulle and Giraud at the end of the Casablanca Conference
10 Roosevelt with Generalissimo Chiang-Kai-shek in Cairo, 1943
11 The chief photo opportunity at the Cairo Conference
12 Churchill convalescing in North Africa, 1943, is visited by Generals Eisenhower and Alexander
13 Canadian Prime Minister Mackenzie King listens to an exchange between Prime Minister Churchill and President Roosevelt in Quebec City

Illustrations

14 Churchill's sixty-ninth birthday party at Teheran, 1943
15 Eleanor Roosevelt and Clementine Churchill broadcasting together at the Quebec Conference of 1944
16 Winston and Clementine cheered by troops on the *Queen Mary*
17 Stalin greets Churchill's daughter Sarah at Teheran
18 Roosevelt meeting with Stalin without Churchill
19 Roosevelt with Soviet Foreign Minister Molotov at Yalta
20 An ailing Roosevelt and a sceptical Churchill at Yalta

PICTURE CREDIT

All illustrations courtesy of the Imperial War Museum, London.

Acknowledgements

In writing this book I have been helped by a number of institutions and individuals.

My greatest obligation by far is to my wife Joan Hardwick who took time from working on her book to type my manuscript and to do the greater part of the index. She has also advised, encouraged and sustained me at every stage of the writing.

I am also grateful for the assistance of my son Benjamin Alldritt who is very knowledgeable about the Second World War and who has supplied me with a great deal of insight and information.

Like anyone writing about this subject I am indebted to the pioneering scholarship of Martin Gilbert and Warren F. Kimball.

I thank the Social Sciences and Humanities Research Council of Canada for financial support for work on this book.

I am also grateful for the facilities provided by the Department of Photographs at the Imperial War Museum, the Library of the University of British Columbia, the Library of the City of Vancouver, the Lichfield Library and the London Library.

Introduction

This book is about friendship. It describes how this particular possibility in human experience is instanced in the singular relationship between two of the greatest political geniuses of the first half of this century. A friendship is always created by a context: a neighbourhood, a career, a hobby, a cause. That between Franklin Roosevelt and Winston Churchill was brought about initially by the coming of the Second World War and the resulting political and military alliance between Britain and the United States. The relationship between the two men was necessitated by history. But it also developed strengths and depths beyond what history demanded but which in turn became a force in and upon history.

My background as a writer is not that of a military or political historian but that of a literary critic, novelist and biographer. And what I offer here is not one more study of Roosevelt and Churchill in terms of large issues of world politics, strategy or of the larger historical forces which they may be seen to direct or be directed by. Rather I have attempted, primarily, to tell the story of this friendship in its human actuality as it developed over the years. Bearing in mind there are generations of readers who have grown up since the end of the Second World War I have tried to go beyond names and abstractions and to evoke the two men and those around them as the characters they were. I have tried to establish the psychological and social make-up of the two men, the rhythms of their friendship, their different styles of humour, their egotisms, the food and drink they shared (lots of that!), the semiotics of the way they dressed, the effect on them of the locations (on three different continents) in which they met.

Churchill and Roosevelt were both schooled in the classical history of ancient Rome and Greece; it was one of the many bonds between them. And as a way of contextualising particular occasions in the course of the Second World War they would often refer to stories of ancient heroes. And I shall tell their story in the war, which was the greatest war in the history of this planet, as a story of the friendship of two heroic men who were at the centre of an epic story. Of course their relationship cannot be seen in isolation; numerous and complex forces bore upon them. An important condition of it was the milieu created by the lesser and minor characters, the advisers and experts and courtiers and cronies that each of them had. The story is one of patriarchy, a singular and epic story of elderly male bonding within a larger group of middle aged and elderly men. Women only appear in the narrative when the central friendship is firmly established. Though it is clear that in Roosevelt's case the strong wish for male bonding was in part created by complex and painful difficulties he had with his wife and with other women.

A friendship is a process in time, an interaction, a dialectic. It is an ongoing pleasure in compatibilities and a continuing reconciliation of incompatibilities. In the case of Roosevelt and Churchill the reasons for sympathy are readily apparent. In a North Atlantic world which they saw threatened by the excited, fanatical leaders from working-class origins such as Hitler and Mussolini they were composed and worldly aristocrats. They had the easy confidence of members of families long accustomed to social standing and to power. The Roosevelts had been squires in Hyde Park in rural New York State for generations and the Oyster Bay branch of the family had already produced one United States President in Teddy Roosevelt. Winston Churchill, historian and writer, was ever mindful not only of his politically flamboyant father but also of his great ancestor, the first Duke of Marlborough, the renowned victor over the armies of Louis XIV. Also Churchill and Roosevelt were White Anglo-Saxon Protestants. And they were of their generation. They were unselfconscious elitists. They were connoisseurs of the English language, of food and drink, of jokes, stories and ironies. They were unreflecting racists. Together they became good old boys with much style.

Yet each man had characteristics and attitudes that could quickly put him at odds with the other. Churchill was a dyed in the wool imperialist in his political assumptions and in his actions. It was one of the ways in which Roosevelt was so very much an American that he envisioned and sought to create a new and post-imperial world order. Indeed the post-colonial world in which we now believe ourselves to be is something which he significantly helped to create. But in so doing he found the friendship with Churchill often put under great strain. Humanly and politically Roosevelt was even prepared for his own ends to risk his friendship with Churchill and exert his famous charm to build an understanding with Stalin. One of the most difficult phases in the friendship began when Roosevelt, always massively confident of his ability to manage men, wooed Stalin by making a fool of Churchill. Incidents of betrayal and jealousy were experiences the friendship had to assimilate and survive.

The years in which the Churchill–Roosevelt relationship developed were ones in which there was much greater difference than now between Britain and the United States in manners, dress, style, vocabulary and idiom. As we observe the process of the friendship as Roosevelt and Churchill experienced it, we are very aware of this difference, with Roosevelt habitually more relaxed, cool, informal, laid back. The contrast, and at times the conflict between these personal styles is one of the things that gives the relationship interest in terms of western social history. And for all that I have, in this book, tried to emphasise and to vivify the human particularities of the friendship, it has to be said that it was also a matter of western history and of practical power politics at the same time that it was something of great pleasure and importance to two remarkable individual human beings. As we trace their story we are also tracing, inevitably, the story of the greatest war in the history of the world, and one which was to settle the world order for almost the remainder of this century. That Roosevelt and Churchill had such an impact on these historic years is, in considerable part, due to the fact that they had a friendship. A friendship can be a solace, a pleasure, a support, a diversion; the story of Franklin Roosevelt and Winston Churchill together shows how friendship can be a power.

Prelude

Friendship between mortals can be contracted on no other terms
than that one must sometime mourn for the other's death.
                              Samuel Johnson, *The Rambler*, Number 17.

In the last week of March 1945, the President of the
United States, haggard, ill and close to total exhaustion,
could stand to be in the political hurly burly of
Washington D.C. no longer. He fled first to Hyde Park,
the mansion and estate on the bluffs over the Hudson
River, not far from Poughkeepsie, which was his home as
it had been that of his Roosevelt forebears who had lived
and grown wealthy in the state of New York for nearly
three centuries. Back in his family home the President
received good news about the world war: American
forces had taken the island of Iwo Jima from the Japanese,
the British under General Montgomery had successfully
crossed the Rhine and were advancing into Germany and
General Patton's tanks were moving into Bavaria. But the
sick President could scarcely take it in. Hyde Park had
been no cure. Desperate about his weakness and his
inability to concentrate and think and act as President he
now demanded that he be taken from this imposing old
house from which he had launched his campaigns for
Governor of New York and, four times, for President of
the United States. He now insisted on going to the place

where his health had been improved years before. This was his other home in Warm Springs in the western part of the State of Georgia.

Roosevelt had first gone to Warm Springs some twenty years before. It was then a run down little resort town, known for its beneficial waters, in which one of Franklin Roosevelt's wealthy friends had a financial interest. At that time Roosevelt had been crippled by polio for some three years. He had first been afflicted by the illness some months after he had run as the Democratic Vice-Presidential Candidate in November 1920. On that first visit to Warm Springs in the beautiful autumn of 1924, the water there had a beneficial effect on his damaged legs. He had made return visits and in 1926 decided to buy the resort, paying just over two hundred thousand dollars from his personal fortune. A year later Franklin Roosevelt founded the Georgia Warm Springs Foundation which was to assist polio sufferers like himself and also other physically disadvantaged people. He invited contributions from the many rich people he had come to know since his schooldays at Groton, his undergraduate years at Harvard, his time as New York State Senator in Albany and eight years as a promising young Democratic politician in Washington, in the administration of Woodrow Wilson. Roosevelt who in his home community of Hyde Park had very much the role of the English squire was a natural paternalist and quickly built up a community of handicapped people at Warm Springs. Visitors to the little spa town in the early thirties were surprised to come upon this unusual township in which everyone had a serious physical disadvantage and in which important sporting events were softball games between polio patients in their wheelchairs and their physiotherapists who, to make for a fair game, played on crutches with their ankles tied.

Roosevelt's enthusiasm for life at Warm Springs was not shared by his wife Eleanor. Well to the left of her husband politically the forceful Eleanor Roosevelt could not tolerate the segregation and racism to be found in small town Georgia at that time. Eleanor was a prohibitionist, a feminist, a liberal, a woman of good family from the North. Her marriage to Franklin Roosevelt in 1905 when she was nineteen and he twenty-three came about in a way that could have been part of one of Edith Wharton's novels of New York high society in the Edwardian age. A niece of the Republican President, Teddy Roosevelt, Eleanor had been brought up to be sceptical about the South. And Warm Springs confirmed her preconceptions. She was especially uncomfortable with the poverty, particularly the black poverty of rural Georgia and with what she regarded as its slow, self-indulgent style of life and speech.

Roosevelt's liking for the South and his political accommodations with Southern Democrats were not the only things that made for distance, uneasiness, awkwardness between himself and his characterful wife. Far more estranging was Under Secretary Roosevelt's affair, beginning in 1917, with Eleanor's secretary, the strikingly beautiful, twenty two year old socialite from Baltimore, Lucy Mercer. After months of bitter discussions between husband and wife sometimes involving family members, Franklin finally agreed to renounce Lucy. Divorce, he recognised, would ruin his political prospects and, at the same time, prevent him from marrying Lucy who was from a Catholic family. He promised never to see Lucy again. But he did not keep his word. Even when Lucy in her late twenties had married Mr Winthrop Rutherford, a wealthy fifty-six-year-old widower with five children, she still communicated occasionally with her first love. Winthrop Rutherford, who also belonged to Edith

Wharton's world and was indeed the prototype of several of the heroes of her early novels, was a man of considerable social standing who bred horses and fox terriers. When he died, he left his young wife an estate called Tranquility near Allamuchy in western New Jersey and a plantation estate near Aiken in South Carolina.

On March 30th, 1945, exactly a calendar month before Adolf Hitler and Eva Braun committed suicide together in the bunker underneath the Reich's Chancellory in Berlin, Franklin Roosevelt with his servants, his doctor and secret service men arrived, as he had insisted, in Warm Springs. The President was now so ill that at times he could scarcely stay conscious. But in his periods of lucidity there was one thing he was determined upon. He wanted Lucy Mercer to come over from nearby Aiken and stay with him. His wife, Eleanor, was not to know of this, any more than she had known of other such meetings.

Lucy agreed to come, in just over a week's time. She also asked if she might have a portrait painted of him. If he agreed she would bring with her the fashionable portrait painter Elizabeth Shoumatoff. Roosevelt quickly consented. After a day or two he began to feel much better. As on earlier occasions Warm Springs helped to restore him. In those afternoons of late spring he would have himself driven through the burgeoning Georgian countryside. He was charmed by the deep blue of the skies and by the peach orchards in blossom. Before a week was out, he was able to take up a few of his Presidential tasks and to interest himself again in the world of politics and male bonding in which he felt more composed and secure than in his marital, sexual and familial relationships. Franklin Roosevelt's relations with women, especially with his wife, were extremely important to him and yet difficult and often painful. His several friendships with men, including the historic one with Winston Churchill, were easier sources of reassurance and well being.

As he awaited Lucy Mercer during those early April days, Roosevelt also interested himself in the San Francisco Conference scheduled to start in the last week of the month. The purpose of the Conference was to draw up the Charter of the United Nations. As a one time Woodrow Wilson Democrat who had been greatly saddened by the fate of the League of Nations which had been created at the end of the First World War, the President had high hopes of this new organisation which was in great part his initiative. He planned to attend the opening session of the Conference. Roosevelt was a keen stamp collector and during these same days of recuperation he spent a good deal of time designing a U.S. postage stamp to commemorate the founding of the new organisation.

Roosevelt was also interested in genealogy, particularly the genealogy of the Roosevelts. And he liked to preside over gatherings of the family and the clan. So a couple of days before Lucy arrived he was happy to receive two of his cousins, Margaret Suckley and Laura Delano. As the two ladies entered his spacious, pleasant cottage among the pine trees they were shocked to see how thin and weak Franklin seemed. His famous good looks, the fine set eyes, the broad cheek bones, the strong jaw had virtually disappeared under white, sagging skin. His hands shook violently as he mixed cocktails for them. And when he tried to pour the drinks from the mixer he greatly embarrassed himself by knocking the glasses on to the floor.

When Lucy Mercer at last arrived, she too was taken aback by Franklin's changed appearance. But she put a brave face on her distress, telling her companion, the fashionable portraitist, 'Mopsy' Shoumatoff, that, having lost so much weight, Franklin looked the way he did when she had first known him well over a quarter of a century before. For Roosevelt Lucy had hardly changed at all since those distant turbulent times. She was still trim, elegantly dressed, with a beautiful even face and fine, blue eyes, the only noticeable change was the partial silvering of her light brown hair.

The President was greatly at his ease sitting talking to her in the sunny sitting room of his cottage and driving with her in the spring countryside. On the second day of her stay he had his cooks, who were lodged in some of the nearby resort cottages, prepare a special meal in her honour. The President's butler, Arthur Prettyman and the Philippino houseboy waited on the table pouring wine, as the party ate veal and noodles and then a waffle with whipped cream and chocolate sauce. The following day, April 12th, the President was to sit for his portrait. Happy to keep his promise to Lucy, he made a great impression the next morning when he was wheeled into the sitting room no longer dressed in a sweater and slacks but in very formal clothes. He wore a double-breasted grey suit and striking tie of crimson silk. He made a strong effort to be debonair and good humoured. He had himself positioned beside one of the windows that gave on to the pine trees. As Mopsy Shoumatoff adjusted her easel and started to paint, Lucy chatted happily to the sitter. Lucy's attitude to the President was, as always, gentle, admiring, solicitous. Using Windsor blue Margaret Shoumatoff roughed in the deep shadows on her subject's face. In his emaciated features she began to detect the handsome looks which over the years had so attracted women voters. She worked steadily and there was a pleasant calm in the sunny room.

But then suddenly the President made a violent awkward movement in his wheelchair. He passed his hand jerkily over his head. As if trying to apologise, but obviously in acute pain he gasped, 'I have a terrible headache.' And then he slumped forward in his chair, unconscious.

Lucy Mercer Rutherford stood up, terrified. After a moment's hesitation she turned and ran from the room to fetch the President's doctor. Elizabeth Shoumatoff dropping her brushes hurried after her. Within minutes the two women returned with the doctor who quickly and nervously felt the President's heart and breathing, his head and his torso and his throat, stripping off the new silk tie. In shock himself the doctor told the two onlookers that the President's condition was critical.

Lucy Mercer was in an agony of distress and uncertainty but soon decided that she and Elizabeth must leave. Whatever was to happen, it would be to the President's discredit if the press were to discover her there. Utterly distraught and with Elizabeth's arm about her she left the cottage, staggered to her car and was driven away.

Arthur Prettyman and the Philippino houseboy then carried the unconscious President from his wheelchair to his bed in an adjacent room. After a more extended and thorough checking of his patient, the doctor diagnosed a massive cerebral haemorrhage. The President's face and head discoloured to a deep purple; his doctor stayed with him. At just half past three, Central Time, on the day the American Third Army captured the historic German city of Weimar, Franklin Delano Roosevelt, President of the United States and acknowledged leader of the western alliance was pronounced dead.

About the time the President died, Prime Minister Winston Churchill was at dinner at his favourite London club and his guest was the President's adviser, associate and contributor to Democratic Party funds, Bernard

Baruch. This vastly wealthy New York speculator who had come from humble origins had been friends with the British Prime Minister for many years. In the great crash on Wall Street in 1929 when Churchill lost most of his money and set off to Hollywood to try to sell film scripts to Charlie Chaplin, Bernard Baruch had entertained him lavishly in his luxury apartment on Fifth Avenue in New York and had tried to help him set himself to rights financially. But their relationship went back even further than that, to a time when Baruch was financial adviser to President Woodrow Wilson and went to Britain at the end of the First World War to discuss economic matters with members of the Lloyd George government in which Churchill was a senior minister.

Churchill always admired the worldliness and frankness of Bernard Baruch. And when Churchill dropped him off at the American Embassy after dinner that evening it is unlikely that the New York financier left him in any doubt concerning Roosevelt's health and prospects. And yet when the news reached him, the Prime Minister was devastated. After parting from Baruch he was driven to the Downing Street Annexe. These were austere underground rooms (now known as the War Rooms) beneath a government building in Whitehall to which Churchill and his staff removed to escape the German bombing and subsequent V1 and V2 rocket attacks. Here that April night Churchill sat at his modest desk sipping brandy and painstakingly working through a stack of government documents and the complex political issues they involved. Churchill was a heavy drinker but few ever spoke of him as an alcoholic. But a workaholic he surely was, all the time bringing his immense energy to bear on even the smallest points of administration, war strategy and world politics. That spring night amidst the makeshift office furniture of the

Annexe and under its harsh electric light, the small hunched figure with the bald head worked and drank until long after midnight. Then a very young officer, one of his aides, approached him uneasily, to give him the bad news from Warm Springs, Georgia.

For all the forewarnings Churchill was knocked sideways by what he was told. He paced about the concrete floor speaking of the loss in highly emotional terms, as his uniformed assistants and secretaries looked on. Tears came into his eyes. He continued to pace. He would not settle. He had the news telegraphed to his wife, Clementine, who was on a goodwill journey to the Soviet Union. Then he paced again, all the time sipping brandy. Finally and miserably he went to bed in his small, rudimentary underground bedroom but could not sleep. He got up early and to the naval officer who was the first of his aides to come to him, he tried to explain himself by saying, with slow, painful deliberation, 'I am much weakened in every way by his loss.'

Four days after he received the news of Roosevelt's death, Churchill attended the great memorial service for the President which he arranged to be held in St Paul's Cathedral in the City of London. After this he went on to the House of Commons to speak of his dead friend and of their relationship. Some, of course, saw this relationship as, at best, a political necessity for both men. And some cynics, as they saw Churchill weeping uncontrollably as he stood outside St Paul's Cathedral on that bright April morning, saw his tears as a piece of self indulgence, an appeal for sympathy, a publicity stunt. One of these was Sir Henry 'Chips' Channon, one of the several brilliant diarists to chronicle the war years in Britain. Henry Channon had large resources of cynicism. He was an American social adventurer from Chicago who, after Oxford, had been the lover of the French novelist, Marcel

Proust, then gone on to marry a titled Guiness heiress, to become more British than the British and to serve as Tory M.P. for the working-class seaside resort of Southend-on-Sea. During the 1930s he had been one of the prominent appeasers of Hitler and the Nazis in the House of Commons. He was well received in Berlin and greatly enjoyed the hospitality of Ribbentrop and Goering.

As 'Chips' Channon and his son left the great baroque cathedral after the memorial service and set off down Ludgate Hill they looked back and saw a sight which Channon later described with some pointed irony. He wrote, 'turning back towards St Paul's we saw Winston standing bare-headed, framed between two columns of the portico, and he was sobbing as the shaft of sunlight fell on his face and the cameras clicked.'[1] The implication is that Churchill's emotional response to the death of Roosevelt was a matter of furthering an image, that is to say, something for the media. And the further implication is that genuine personal feeling was not involved. But this was to be denied by Churchill later that day when he went to the House of Commons to speak of his friendship with Roosevelt. He spoke of it then as a major experience in his personal as well as his political life.

On that day of mourning, when he spoke in the House of Commons Churchill could but generalise, and at no great length, about the history of his long and historic relationship with the President. His passionate eulogy was a condensation of all that happened between them. In the following pages I will attempt to tell the story in detail, to trace the origins and development and to describe the pains, pleasures and achievements deriving from this complex friendship between two egotistical men of genius.

The very first meeting between Franklin Roosevelt and

Winston Churchill did not go well. It took place in 1918 when President Woodrow Wilson's handsome and rather vain Under Secretary of the Navy went with a delegation representing the government, the army and the navy of the United States to co-ordinate with the British America's military contribution to the winning of the First World War. One official function to which the visiting Americans were invited was a reception at Grays Inn, one of the Inns of Court where British lawyers and barristers had trained since at least the fifteenth century. The American guests were duly impressed by the Great Hall famous for its beautiful painted ceiling which dated back to the end of the seventeenth century. Here the Americans sat to hear several speeches including one by the forty-four-year-old Winston Churchill, then a Liberal M.P. and Minister of Munitions and a senior member of the coalition government headed by the Welsh Liberal Prime Minister, David Lloyd George. Franklin Roosevelt, eight years younger than the flamboyant Churchill and very much his junior in political rank and experience, was intrigued to meet this controversial and colourful figure.

For the seemingly genteel squire of Hyde Park on the Hudson Churchill's origins seemed to belong to melodrama. Churchill's father had been Lord Randolph Churchill, a son of the Duke of Marlborough and the eloquent, brilliant proponent of 'Tory Democracy' in late Victorian England. This charismatic aristocrat had married Jennie Jerome of New York City, the daughter of the kind of wealthy but raffish Manhattan speculator whom the Roosevelts of Hyde Park would definitely decline 'to know'. When Winston was twenty, his father had died discredited and mad. Lord Randolph's widow, Jennie, then engaged in a series of love affairs including one with Bourke Cockran, a wealthy Irish American who was a power in Tammany Hall in New York City, a political organisation within the Democratic Party which one day would be an obstacle and an embarrassment to an upstate Democrat such as Franklin Roosevelt. But Winston Churchill was to remember Cockran as one who taught him a good deal about both politics and oratory.

It was not just his parentage that made the young Winston Churchill such a high profile figure in the press of Britain and America. Right from the outset his own life had been extremely eventful. As a gifted writer he was able and keen to publicise himself. After he had completed his military training and graduated from Sandhurst, he had been an army officer and then a war correspondent first in India and then in South Africa during the Boer War. Here he had gained his first headlines by making a dramatic escape from a Boer prisoner of war camp. (In later years Roosevelt, very much an anti-imperialist, would kid Churchill a great deal about his role in this first war, in the twentieth century, for liberation from the British Empire.) His feat in South Africa and the fame it brought him helped Churchill to be elected to the House of Commons as a Tory M.P. And then within a few years he was back on the front pages when he spectacularly 'crossed the floor' of the House, leaving the Tory Party, in which he had been born and raised, and joining the Liberal opposition. After his new party came to power in 1905 Churchill was given government office and quickly promoted. When the First World War began in 1914, he was First Lord of the Admiralty, a position which, in those days when sea power was of crucial importance, was one of the key jobs in the British government. (An important bond between Churchill and Roosevelt was that each had had the power and the responsibility for his country's navy. Churchill's identifying himself as 'Former Naval Person' in his messages to Roosevelt was a regular reminder of this shared experience.)

In 1915 Churchill as First Lord of the Admiralty again gained notoriety when he promoted the military expedition to the Dardanelles in Turkey. This was an attempt to resolve the deadlock of the trench warfare in France by opening up a second front in the East. The initiative was a total disaster. The Liberal government lost confidence. And Churchill's old associates, the Tories, made it a condition of their joining a coalition government with the Liberals that Churchill, the political failure, and also the hated renegade, should be removed from high office. Churchill left the Admiralty and later spent some time in the trenches in France. But eventually his old political ally, David Lloyd George, who had become the Prime Minister of the coalition government managed to wangle him back into government. In the last year of the war Churchill was a forceful, energetic Minister of Munitions.

So the short, burly, pugnacious man who rose to speak in the seventeenth century Hall of Grays Inn that day in 1918 had far more of a political track record than Under Secretary Roosevelt whose career, prior to his appointment to a junior position in the administration of President Woodrow Wilson as Under Secretary of the Navy had been confined to the politics of the state of New York. As Churchill rose to speak, Roosevelt, like the other Americans, had a strong sense of anticipation. To hear this flamboyant superstar of British politics, already famous for his oratory, would surely be an experience. But Churchill's speech that day was not a success. The Americans found his attitude to them to be pompous, patronising, even dictatorial. They, he implied, were Johnnies Come Lately in a war which Britain had fought for nearly four years. The Americans clearly needed British wisdom, know-how, direction.

Some time before this speech the novelist H.G. Wells

who, more than once, used Churchill as a character in his novels, described him as part pushy American and part reactionary, bullying Prussian aristocrat, or Junker (pronounced Yunker). Churchill was, said Wells, a Yankee-Yunker. And it was this side of his complex character which impressed and annoyed his guests on that grand occasion in 1918 which had been organised to create good will and to help strengthen the alliance. After the speech which so many of the Americans found slighting, things got worse. As Churchill was introduced to the American guests individually, he made it plain that he had somewhere to go on to. His manner to them was perfunctory, even curt. They could be in no doubt that he regarded these introductions as tiresome but unavoidable formalities. Under Secretary Roosevelt who regarded himself as an American grandee and as a man of great promise both in his party and in his country was irritated and offended by the barely concealed indifference which the British Minister showed towards him.

Roosevelt never forgot the incident; Churchill did but, over two decades later, felt it necessary to pretend that he had been greatly impressed by the Under Secretary for the United States Navy.

In the decade following the First World War both men would experience personal and political calamity. With the marginalisation of the Liberal Party in Britain in the early 1920s Churchill was for some time without a seat in Parliament. Motivated in great part by his rabid, sometimes hysterical hostility to the Bolshevik regime in Russia, he returned to the Tory Party and as Chancellor of the Exchequer held one of the highest positions in the government. But in 1929 the Labour Party took over as the ruling party and Churchill lost office. He also lost most of his money in the Wall Street Crash. At times during the thirties he and his wife had difficulties coping with their debts at the butcher's and grocer's. Often in deep depression Churchill retreated into his hobbies: painting and bricklaying.

In 1921 Franklin Roosevelt was afflicted by the poliomyelitis that virtually deprived him of the use of his legs for the rest of his life. But with intense determination he struggled to overcome this disadvantage and gradually managed to rebuild his political career. In this he was much assisted by the former race track reporter and gifted political manager, the gnome-like Louis B. Howe, one of a succession of men who were compelled by Roosevelt's magnetism and his remarkable charm. In the year of the great financial crash as Churchill worried about his financial losses Roosevelt became Governor of his native state and four years later as the economic Depression grew worse, he became President of the United States. His 'New Deal' was his means of seeking to revitalise the American economy. It entailed a variety of government initiatives, programmes and involvements in the social and financial system. He campaigned for it vigorously, making effective use of his communications concept of the 'fireside chat' on radio. One of Roosevelt's distinctions was that he was pre-eminently the President of the radio age.

Much of the energy impelling the 'New Deal' derived from another close and intense friendship. This was with Harry Hopkins, a Midwesterner who came from a humble background in small town Iowa. After graduating college, the tense idealistic, energetic Hopkins had become a social worker and then an administrator of social programmes in New York. Here this future hero of the left wing of the Democratic Party had come to the notice of Roosevelt's supporters and then of the President himself. The cool, urbane patrician from upstate New York and the homely, chain smoking dedicated social missionary from

31

Grinnell, Iowa, quickly took to each other. And as they led the New Deal together, they drew ever closer. Their programme polarised America. Many (and in 1936 an electoral majority) felt a passionate admiration for them and their policies: among others there was doubt and among Conservatives, a passionate hatred of Hopkins and his politically skilful patron whom they called 'that snakecharmer in the White House'.

The year after Roosevelt's inauguration as President, Winston Churchill, a British Conservative long considered a spent force and consigned to his party's back benches in the House of Commons and now eking out a precarious living by his writing, had an ambivalent attitude towards Roosevelt and the New Deal. In an essay to which he gave the title 'Roosevelt From Afar' he first conceded the enormity of the crisis which faced the new President.

> He arrived at the summit of the greatest economic community in the world at the moment of its extreme embarrassment. Everybody had lost faith in everything. Credit was frozen. Millions of unemployed without provision filled the streets or wandered despairing about the vast spaces of America. The rotten foundations of the banks were simultaneously undermined and exposed. A universal deadlock gripped the United States. The richest man could not cash the smallest cheque. People possessing enormous intrinsic assets in every kind of valuable security found themselves for some days without the means to pay an hotel bill or even a taxi fare. We must never forget that this was the basis from which he started.[2]

At the same time Churchill expressed his reservations about the implications of the New Deal and what he called 'the vague, ethereal illusions of sentimentalists or doctrinaires'. Clearly as far away as London the old Tory could smell creeping socialism. 'It would be a thousand pities,' he continued, 'if this tremendous effort by the richest nation in the world to expand consciously and swiftly the bounds of the consuming power should be vitiated by being mixed up with an ordinary radical programme and a commonplace class fight'. Three paragraphs from the end of his essay Churchill feels it necessary to warn Roosevelt directly against the runaway tendencies of New Dealers like Hopkins. Of Roosevelt's Presidency he writes, 'Roosevelt will rank among the greatest of men who have occupied that proud position ... But the President has need to be on his guard. To a foreign eye it seems that forces are gathering under his shield which at a certain stage may thrust him into the background and take the lead themselves.'[3]

Did Roosevelt in 1934 know of these warnings from Churchill? Probably not. In the thirties Churchill came to seem more and more of a political dinosaur. His rigid, heavily imperialist views were an important reason that the Conservative controlled governments during most of that decade kept him on the back benches. Also annoying to his colleagues in government were his ever more hostile speeches against the Nazi government that had taken power in Germany in 1933. In the Conservative Party there were many who believed in appeasing Hitler and who found Churchill's denunciations of Nazi policy an embarrassment and a nuisance. There was even an attempt to have him de-selected as a Conservative parliamentary candidate.

But then came Hitler's quick, successful takeovers in Czechoslovakia and Austria. And then the Anglo-French Treaty with Poland failed to deter Hitler from attacking that country. So Britain found itself at war. Suddenly Churchill was seen to be vindicated and the policies of the Conservative Neville Chamberlain, misguided and discredited. Chamberlain tacitly admitted as much when he invited Churchill to come back into government. After ten years as a political has-been the sixty-five year old veteran resumed ministerial office by taking up the very post he had been forced to give up nearly twenty-five years before, that of the First Lord of the Admiralty.

Just eight days after Churchill walked back into the Admiralty, the sturdy eighteenth-century building at the north end of Whitehall, he unexpectedly received a personal message from the President of the United States. President Roosevelt wrote suggesting that they establish and develop a personal contact.

Unquestionably Roosevelt's motive in doing this was one of political self interest. Officially America's policy was to keep out of the war. And with a presidential election due in just over a year's time. Roosevelt continually proclaimed and endorsed this policy. But he disliked what he knew of Fascism in Italy and Germany. And he was mindful of the implications for the United States of Fascist domination in Europe and, possibly, invasion or involvement in the Americas. He decided to take steps to keep himself closely informed about the course of the war. As so often when he contemplated an initiative, Franklin Roosevelt looked to individuals rather than to institutions. In order to have the best insight into events in Europe he did not rely on the State Department or the American Embassy in London or in any other European capital. As in the cases of Louis B. Howe and Harry Hopkins he trusted in a particular man. In this new personal initiative in foreign affairs he chose that one time political prima donna, latterly unemployed but now rehabilitated, Winston Churchill.

For a head of state and of government in one country to propose an informal pen-friendship with a mere member of the government in another was, of course, startlingly unorthodox. But so to personalise politics was very Rooseveltian. The letter he sent was very much he; it was courteous, informal, cool and charming. It began with a personal touch noting that Churchill like himself had had naval responsibilities in the First World War. Then the letter became a little flattering as it expressed admiration for Churchill's four volumes of biography on the subject of his ancestor the first Duke of Marlborough. The President concluded, 'I much enjoyed reading them'. But after such personal pleasantries came the crucial sentence. Carefully, and tactfully, not excluding from his invitation Prime Minister Chamberlain whose political future was however clearly a very bleak one, the President wrote to Churchill, 'What I want you and the Prime Minister to know is that I shall at all times welcome it if you will keep me in touch personally with anything you want me to know about'.[4]

With this one sentence, full of hints, possibilities, suggestion and promise, Roosevelt took a major initiative and the historic friendship began.

Notes

1. Henry Channon, *Diaries*, ed. Robert Rhodes James (Weidenfeld & Nicolson, 1978), p. 317.
2. Winston Churchill, 'Roosevelt From Afar' in *Great Contemporaries* (Odhams, 1948 ed.), p. 295.
3. *Ibid.*, p. 303.
4. Warren F. Kimball, ed., *Churchill And Roosevelt The Complete Correspondence In 3 Volumes* (Princeton University Press, 1984), p. 19.

1 A Pen Friendship

Friendship is only a reciprocal accommodation of interests, and an exchange of good offices; it is a kind of commerce out of which self-love always expects to gain something.

La Rochefoucauld, *Maxims*

Roosevelt had chosen the right man. Churchill wrote back immediately, agreeing to the idea. And if the President initiated the contact, the Englishman from the outset worked hard in every possible way to sustain and develop it. An early and ongoing contribution to these exchanges was Churchill's readiness to serve as the President's entertainer. Roosevelt was fascinated by ships and the sea. (Earlier in his life he had owned and sailed boats. He also collected model ships and had a large collection of them.) Churchill quickly hit on the idea of sending the President in neutral America detailed accounts of sea battles and engagements in which the Royal Navy became involved. Churchill, the biographer, essayist, historian, writer of movie scripts, novelist and autobiographer now took on, early in his new ministerial career, the extra task of becoming a teller of sea stories to an audience of one.

An excellent opportunity for such story telling occurred when, during those early months of the 'phoney war', three British cruisers in the South Atlantic, HMS *Ajax*, *Achilles* and *Exeter* chased the German pocket battleship

Graf Spee into the harbour of Montevideo in neutral Uruguay. International law required that the *Graf Spee* should leave the harbour within twenty-four hours or be interred along with her crew. What would the German captain decide to do? There were hours of suspense. Eventually the commander took the same ultimate decision as the German Admiral, for whom the battleship was named, had done at the Battle of the Falklands in 1914. First he wrote his will on the Nazi battle ensign, then he ordered the *Graf Spee* scuttled. And then he shot himself.

Churchill sent Roosevelt a lengthy account of the action off Montevideo which led up to this conclusion. Later he sent him the official British history of the episode, *The Battle of the River Plate*. Churchill's highly tuned intuition told him that his stories created interest and pleasure. He worked assiduously at them. And when Roosevelt, in the spring of 1941 became unwell and went off on a fishing trip off the coast of Southern Florida, Churchill made even greater efforts to send him accounts of various incidents in the naval war in the Atlantic. To his colleagues in London Churchill, confident and very pleased with himself, remarked, 'This is the kind of stuff he likes on his cruise'.

An affinity between the two correspondents quickly revealed itself. They became keen to meet each other. The exchange of messages was scarcely three months old when Roosevelt, contemplating the growing complexities of the war remarked, 'I wish much [sic] that I could talk things over with you in person.' Churchill showing the respect which, early on in the correspondence he always maintained towards Roosevelt as a head of state, regretted that he could not 'have the honour of talking to you in person'. It would be another eighteen months before their relationship developed significantly with their first face to face meeting. In the intervening year and a half their friendship was a thing of words. But still it grew warmer, even in the midst of dramatically changing circumstances.

In May of 1940 Chamberlain's government fell and Churchill took over as Prime Minister. He immediately wrote to the President, 'Although I have changed my office, I am sure you would not wish me to discontinue our intimate, private correspondence'. And Roosevelt quickly confirmed this. The subsequent exchanges between the two of them are mainly about political, military, financial and strategic matters. Often there is obvious input from their advisers. But there are also more personal touches. On May 16th 1940, the day Churchill flew to Paris to try to invigorate the failing government of France, the theoretically neutral President ends his letter with an emphatic, 'The best of luck to you'. Two weeks later, as France falls and the British Expeditionary Force is evacuated from the beaches of Dunkirk, the President, after thanking Churchill for his account of the Battle of the River Plate, concludes with some words of sympathetic understanding. 'You are much in my thoughts. I need not tell you that.'[1]

However, the developing personal relationship also had its moments of setback. The collapse of France was the first of these. For Churchill and the people of Britain this was a devastating blow. They were stunned when this major ally, one of the great imperial powers, gave up on the war and abjectly asked the Nazis for an armistice, and finally underwent the humiliation rituals of surrendering in the same railway carriage at Compiègne in which the Germans had begged for peace in 1918. Desperately Churchill urged Roosevelt to intervene to head off this calamity; he had high hopes that the President would bring his country into the war to help save France. But neither the Constitution of the United

States (which reserves declarations of war to the Congress) nor, in Roosevelt's view, American public opinion would permit such a step. So Churchill had to look on miserably as the Germans divided up a conquered France into an occupied northern zone and a new and neutral state to the south with the spa town of Vichy as its capital.

Whether from disappointment, anger or depression on Churchill's part, or perhaps all three in turn, his communications with Roosevelt ceased for several weeks.

The Fall of France was just the first of a succession of blows that Churchill and his country had to take during 1940. The summer brought the Battle of Britain when Hitler's Luftwaffe sought to eliminate British air power as a preliminary to shipping an invasion army across the Channel. Next, in the autumn came the Blitz, the German bombing campaign to destroy British cities (Coventry a memorable example) and the factories which sustained the British war effort. While Churchill in what he called his fellow countrymen's 'finest hour' battled on, Franklin Roosevelt in that self-same year of 1940 was fighting a battle of a different kind. He was campaigning to be elected President for the third time in the November elections.

A potent force in American politics in that year were the isolationists, chiefly but by no means exclusively from the Republican states of the Midwest. The zealous, tireless, utterly dedicated organiser of Roosevelt's campaign was also from the Midwest. This was the passionate, chain-smoking idealist in the crumpled suit, Harry Hopkins.

Despite all the political problems presented by this election year, Roosevelt was still sympathetic when on the last day of July Churchill resumed the correspondence with yet another appeal for assistance. The Prime Minister was becoming increasingly agitated by the mounting losses of merchant ships bringing indispensable supplies to the now beleagured British Isles. Churchill appealed to Roosevelt for the use of some old American destroyers to help protect the supply ships. Roosevelt was inclined to help and a deal was worked out which allowed the British to have the American ships in return for ninety-nine year leases of military facilities in British possessions in the Americas ranging from Newfoundland to British Guyana. The deal was complicated but Roosevelt was able to push it through chiefly because it was a deal and not just a gift. Some of Churchill's former warmth returned to his message when he expressed his thanks to Roosevelt. 'I am so very grateful to you for all the trouble you have been taking and I am so sorry to add to your burden knowing what a good friend you have been to us.'

This message came at the end of August. Some three months later the President won a comfortable victory over his Republican opponent Wendell Wilkie. In defying precedent to win this third term in the White House Roosevelt carried thirty nine of the forty eight states and had the support of some twenty-seven million votes to Wilkie's twenty two. Churchill shared Roosevelt's pleasure in this splendid victory. Certainly Wendell Wilkie had been sympathetic to the idea of helping Britain and belonged to the liberal, cosmopolitan wing of the Republican Party rather than that of the isolationists and non-interventionists. But for Churchill the special personal bond with Roosevelt was a precious asset. The day after the votes were counted, his relief and pleasure burst out in a letter to Roosevelt. 'I did not think it right for me as a Foreigner to express my opinion upon American policies while the election was on, but now I feel you will not mind my saying that I prayed for your success and that I am truly thankful for it.'[2]

These congratulations received no response from Roosevelt. Churchill long pondered this small discourtesy from a man who was habitually courteous. Joseph Lash, a very left wing young man and a much gossiped about protegé of Eleanor Roosevelt with easy access to the White House at that time, later suggested that Roosevelt's coolness was due to the use which during the Presidential election Wendell Wilkie made of Churchill's comments on the New Deal in his thirties journalism.[3] Whether this is true or not the fact remains that the Roosevelt–Churchill relationship, however close it became, could and would contain within it tiffs and small snubs. A slightly comic strain in the story of their friendship is the occasional gentle bumping of two gigantic egos. This was the first.

Yet despite this pinprick Roosevelt's victory remained a great boost for Churchill after the harrowing summer and autumn of 1940. But calamity still threatened. A vast army on the northern coast of France could still invade Britain. Just a month before election day he told the President, 'I cannot feel that the invasion danger is passed.' But he continued hopefully, using the kind of metaphor for Hitler with which he would often seek to amuse Roosevelt, 'The gent has taken off his clothes and put on his bathing suit but the water is getting colder and there is an autumn nip in the air'.

After his re-election Roosevelt felt able to allow his sympathy for the British cause to become more obvious. The following month he began speaking about a programme to assist Britain with its chronic financial difficulties in paying America for all the supplies it needed. At a press conference in Washington that December he spoke to reporters about the need to get rid of 'The silly, foolish old dollar sign'. And two days before the end of that eventful year he made a speech in which, in a famous phrase, he referred to America as 'The arsenal of democracy'. This was the beginning of Roosevelt's Lease–Lend policy, a programme facilitating assistance for Britain which was endorsed by the House of Representatives early in February and by the Senate a month later.

About a week after New Year's Day 1941, the President sent Harry Hopkins to London to study and report back on the situation there. The sympathy, the curiosity and the political need which Churchill and Roosevelt had for each other at this time were now mediated through a colourful and skilful third party. The differences in background and experience between Churchill and Hopkins were, of course, enormous. Politically they were far apart. But they got on extremely well. Churchill talked to Hopkins endlessly, included him in high level British policy meetings, entertained him in his chilly residence at Chequers, took him up on the Air Ministry roof to see and hear one of the bombing attacks on London, travelled with him around factories and army camps reassuring him about the power and the seriousness of the British war effort. (Ambassador Kennedy had sent negative reports to Washington about Britain's will and capacity to fight on in the war.) Quickly there grew up between Churchill and Hopkins a strong affection. In Washington it was reported that 'The first thing that Churchill asks for when he wakes is Harry Hopkins and Harry Hopkins is the last one he sees at night'. To this one member of Roosevelt's cabinet who was in no way deluded about the extent of Churchill's need and hopes of the United States responded by saying, 'Maybe so. But even if the President had sent someone with bubonic plague as his personal representative, Churchill would, nevertheless, see a good deal of him'.

But for all the national interest that each had to represent, it is clear that the good feeling between

Hopkins and Churchill was genuine and intense. When, some years later, Hopkins lost his place as Roosevelt's chief courtier and adviser, Churchill unquestionably felt a deep sympathy for him. Now at the end of January 1941 as Hopkins at the zenith of his influence prepared to return to Washington, Churchill wrote enthusiastically to Roosevelt about his envoy. 'One can easily see why he is so close to you,' the Prime Minister concluded, in a double edged compliment that flattered Hopkins and Roosevelt simultaneously. But like Hopkins's reports it helped reassure Roosevelt in his vanity concerning Churchill's attitude to him. A couple of months later, when at a dinner for the White House press corps, the President of still neutral America reciprocated by referring to Churchill, the political head of a belligerent state as 'a brilliant and a great leader'.

However, British cities still burned, more and more freighters with essential foodstuffs were sunk in the North Atlantic and the German invasion army was still camped across the Channel. Towards the end of January Roosevelt made another and very personal gesture of friendship and encouragement to Churchill as his country's 'darkest hour' continued. Wendell Wilkie, the defeated Republican candidate in the previous November, now paid a visit to Britain and in his care Roosevelt sent to Churchill, well known as a man of letters, a passage of poetry which he, Roosevelt had copied out in his own hand. For all its rhetoric the passage was clearly intended, and certainly received, as an expression of sympathy and support. The five lines of poetry were from 'Building of the Ship' by the American nineteenth-century poet Henry Wadsworth Longfellow. Less than a year before Pearl Harbor the President wrote, 'I think this verse applies to your people as it does to us.' The lines ran:

> Thou, too sail on, O Ship of State!
> Sail on, O Union, strong and great!
> Humanity with all its fears,
> With all the hope of future years,
> Is hanging breathless on thy fate!

Churchill replied saying that he was 'Deeply moved by the verse of Longfellow's which you quoted'. He went on to write of the special quality which he thought their relationship, so far made up of their exchanges of telegraphs, had begun to develop. In this wire Churchill alluded to 'Our friendly relations which have been built up telegraphically but also telepathically under all the stresses'.[4] This suggestion that he related to Roosevelt telepathically comes close to the notion of their friendship as a mystique as well as a matter of rational alignment of common interests in such matters as geo-politics, strategy, diplomacy and finance. As time went by both came to believe more and more in this mystique. It became one pole of an ongoing interplay, or dialectic, within the friendship; the other pole was the claims of national interest (often articulated by their advisers) together with the claims of personal political advantage and vanity.

And, of course, that sympathetic 'telepathic' sense which each had of the other could be affected, challenged, and then always further refined, by the ongoing actualities of the war. This happened in the spring and summer of 1941, as it had happened about a year before at the time of the Fall of France. On this later occasion British defeats in Greece and North Africa appeared to Churchill to have led Roosevelt 'quite unconsciously' to have lost confidence in Britain as a sustainable ally. To a senior British colleague Churchill surmised, 'It seems to me as if there has been a considerable recession across the Atlantic, and that quite unconsciously we are being left to our own fate'. So in a radio broadcast which he knew would be studied by the President, he offered another poem, surely in answer to the one the President had sent him. He quoted four lines by the Victorian poet Arthur Clough that served to suggest the long term power of the British (imaged as 'the main' or the ocean) despite a time of short term setbacks.

> For while the tired waves, vainly breaking,
> Seem here no painful inch to gain,
> Far back, through creeks and inlets making,
> Comes silent, flooding in, the main.

Churchill's response to Roosevelt's seeming lack of confidence was not confined to subtle poetic suggestions. He could also hector Roosevelt in heavy rhetorical language as if he were addressing a public meeting. In one of his telegrams he warns, 'But I adjure, Mr President, not to underrate the gravity of the consequences ...' Within days the personal tone and touch returned. The relationship was restored anew as Roosevelt ended his wire with the conspicuous, emphatic (if ungrammatical) sentence. 'With this messages goes my warm personal regards to you.'

A rare British success at this time was the sinking of the large, immensely powerful German battleship, the *Bismarck*. This was done by a group of British battleships including a very new one, HMS *Prince of Wales*, commissioned just about a year before. Roosevelt congratulated Churchill warmly on this major naval achievement. 'All of us are made very happy,' he messaged from Washington, 'by the fine tracking down of the *Bismarck* and that she has literally gone for good'. Churchill quickly responded with yet another literary allusion, one that expressed Churchill's overwhelming desire for Roosevelt and the United States to involve themselves in the war in which by no means everything was going well for Britain. After commenting on the British defeat on the island of Crete Churchill recommended that the President open his Bible and read verse two of the sixth chapter of the Second Epistle to the Corinthians. (Such numerical allusions to passages in the Bible offering worldly wisdom came to be a game they very much liked to play together in their exchanges.) If the President read this one, he could be in no doubt what the Prime Minister wanted him to say. 'I have heard thee in a time accepted, and in the day of salvation have I succoured thee: behold now is the accepted time; behold now is the day of salvation.'

But still Roosevelt did not and could not make such a declaration. Europe was no longer the dominant problem for American foreign policy that it had been. Roosevelt was becoming increasingly occupied with the expansionism of the Japanese in the Pacific. And then in the June of that year came one of the decisive events in the history of the Second World War; Hitler attacked the Soviet Union. Winston Churchill the old hater of the Bolsheviks, the supporter and provisioner of the Whites in the struggle against the Reds in the Russian revolution, was happy enough to have a new ally in the struggle against Hitler. Any new ally was good news. Britain no longer stood alone. On that summer day as the German panzers raced into the Ukraine Churchill commented, 'If Hitler invaded Hell, I would at least make a favourable reference to the Devil in the House of Commons'.

The entry of Russia into the war immediately raised new and difficult questions for Roosevelt and Churchill. How should the two free enterprise countries relate to the new communist ally? Should the Russians be sent supplies? If so, how much? And how could they best be delivered? What would western public opinion make of aid to communist Russia? These were questions that were now added to those long emerging ones that Churchill and Roosevelt had still to answer: the response to the activities of the Japanese, differences between the British and Americans in dealing with Vichy France, the problems of administering the recently legislated Lend Lease Programme. The need for Churchill and Roosevelt to have that personal meeting they had talked about months before now became even more compelling. And three weeks after Stalin entered the war, Roosevelt made up his mind to set up such a meeting with Churchill. He sent Harry Hopkins back to London to start making arrangements for it. While these were underway Hopkins went on a freezing dangerous flight to Moscow around the tip of Norway in order to visit Stalin and talk about the prospects for the Soviet war effort. Ill and tormented by the cold Hopkins flew back to Britain just in time to join Churchill as the Prime Minister set off to meet Roosevelt. He found Churchill doing extensive research into Roosevelt's life and career, even studying the words of a recent American hit song entitled 'Franklin D. Roosevelt Jones'.

The many and complex arrangements for the meeting of Churchill and Roosevelt were made in the utmost secrecy. Scarcely anyone in London or Washington knew what was going on. The press was not informed. Even senior members of the British and American governments were kept in the dark. The place and time of the rendezvous were top secret.

Notes

1. Kimball, p. 41.
2. Ibid., p. 81.
3. Joseph P. Lash, *Roosevelt and Churchill* (André Deutsch, 1977), pp. 245–7.
4. Kimball, p. 134.

2 Getting to Know You

I hear tell there's a stranger in the Jones household,
Yes Siree, Yes Siree.
I hear tell there's a new arrival six days old,
Yes Siree, Yes Siree
...
With a name like the one that he's got today
When he walks down the street
Folks will say 'Pleased to meet
Mr FRANKLIN D. ROOSEVELT JONES!'
...
With that handle how can he go wrong?
All the folks in the town will agree
He'll be famous as famous as he can be,
How can he be a dud or a stick in the mud
When he's FRANKLIN D. ROOSEVELT JONES?

Sung by Judy Garland in *Babes on Broadway*, 1941

The Germans pushed ever deeper into the Soviet Union.
And the Nazi agenda grew ever more explicit and
dynamic. On the last day of July 1941 the Hitler
government announced their commitment to 'The Final
Solution'. Goering, on orders from the Führer told
Heydrich to begin 'all necessary preparations ... for
bringing about the complete solution of the Jewish
question'.

Two days later in that high summer an English travel

writer working away at his home in peaceful rural Hampshire received an entirely unexpected telephone call from the Minister of Information. This was Churchill's long time friend and political associate, Brendan Bracken, who had saved the Prime Minister from personal bankruptcy and total exclusion from politics in the late thirties. The Minister asked the writer, H.V. Morton, to come and see him in London on urgent business. Morton duly got on the train at the quiet country station nearby and arrived in a London that had smoking bomb craters everywhere. He presented himself at the Ministry in Westminster where he was hurried up the marble stairs and pushed immediately into the Minister's office. Bracken, a big boned, powerful man, forty years old, with a mass of auburn hair, thick horn-rimmed spectacles and a quick, nervous, insistent manner came straightaway to the point.

'I have an extraordinary proposition to put to you. I want you to leave England for three weeks, but I regret to say that I cannot tell you where you are going ... I can only say that if you go you will see history in the making and be present at one of the great moments of the war. Will you go?'

Without a moment's hesitation Henry Morton, a man in late middle age, and intensely patriotic, agreed to go.

Clearly relieved Bracken went on to inform him that he would travel by battleship on a voyage of some seven days and that one of the other passengers would be his fellow writer, the popular novelist of the day, Howard Spring. Like Morton, Spring had begun as a journalist and had worked for years for the Canadian Press baron, Lord Beaverbrook, on the *Evening Standard*. The mission clearly required reportorial skills. But Bracken would say little more. Morton was to report to the Admiralty at eleven o'clock sharp, on the following day. Then he and Howard

Spring would be given their instructions. Bracken curtly ended the interview. Bemused Henry Morton walked through the London streets where dust and a harsh smell of burning still hung over the large gaping bombsites; he felt as though he were in the opening of a spy novel.

When he arrived at the Admiralty that Sunday morning Morton found his literary colleague, Howard Spring, the small, frail novelist already waiting for him, apprehensively. A senior civil servant approached them and announced that they were ordered to report to Marylebone Station within ninety minutes. Someone would meet them there. The two writers managed to find a taxi and they sped through the quiet Sunday streets guessing nervously about what lay in store for them. At the station a ticket collector, who Morton suspected was probably a detective in disguise, directed them to a long passenger train with many sleeping cars. Morton deduced that this meant a trip to the north of Scotland.

In the restaurant car the tables were set elegantly for lunch but the train seemed almost empty. To the consternation of a rather nervous Howard Spring the near ghost train suddenly jolted into motion, then quickly gathered speed as it headed northwards out of London. It climbed the sunny green slopes of the Chiltern Hills and then came to an abrupt halt in the tiny station of the country town of Wendover. And there on the short wooden platform was an astonishing sight. A smiling Winston Churchill wearing his 'rompers' or siren suit of Air Force blue (a single garment of battle dress design with a zip fastener from neck to waist) and sporting a yachting cap was chatting animatedly to a group of companions in military uniform. Among these, Morton the experienced journalist, recognised Sir John Dill, Chief of the Imperial General Staff, Air-Chief Marshal Sir Wilfred Freeman and Admiral Sir Dudley Pound, the First

Sea Lord. In fact virtually all the leaders of Britain's military struggle against Hitler stood on that small old fashioned station platform in rural Buckinghamshire. Also there was Alexander Cadogan, a high official in the Foreign Office and also Professor Lindemann who held the chair of Experimental Philosophy at Oxford University and who had been Churchill's friend and scientific adviser during the Prime Minister's decade of political exile in the thirties. Morton surmised that the party on the platform had come over from the Prime Minister's country home at nearby Chequers.

Churchill and his entourage boarded the train and it set off north again speeding on through the sunny afternoon, into the dusk and then into the night, stopping only occasionally to change its steam locomotive for another freshly coaled one. The train hurried through the darkness of the blackout. As they moved along the corridor the two writers could see Churchill in his compartment sitting under a shaded reading lamp and wearing a pair of reading glasses as he worked intently at his despatch cases and boxes. He worked on, with characteristic industriousness, long after the others on the train had gone to their bunks. When the travellers awoke on the following morning they found themselves on the misty, rocky coast of northern Scotland due south of the Orkney Islands. At the bleak harbour town of Thurso they were taken out to a destroyer that transported them out to sea. Then out of the mist there gradually emerged the vast towering shape of a battleship. It was HMS *Prince of Wales* recently repaired (though not completely) after being heavily damaged in the action against the giant German battleship *Bismarck*.

As Churchill and his companions clambered aboard the *Prince of Wales* a slight figure stepped forward from the shadow of one of the great gun turrets. It was Harry

Hopkins, ill and emaciated, who had flown straight to the battleship from Moscow after a couple of days' discussion with Stalin. Churchill greeted him warmly and linked arms with him, in his old-fashioned Edwardian way. Preoccupied with their exchanges of news, the pair entered one of the hatchways and went below.

As *Prince of Wales* set off into the Atlantic it was soon hit by a violent storm. Churchill's several journeys to meet Roosevelt were often made in most uncomfortable conditions but the voyage in the great battleship was among the worst. H.V. Morton was quite unable to sleep. 'I climbed into my bunk, but sleep was out of the question. The noise was indescribable; the vibration so persistent that all my books, shaving things, hair brushes and such like, had jumped to the cabin floor where they rolled a foot to port and a foot to starboard with the movement of the ship. The battleship descended into the sea like a falling lift, to rise with surprising buoyancy and slide forward before settling down into the water again.' He went on:

> The monstrous plunges of a great battleship are so deliberate and slow as to be unlike the movement of any other ship, indeed they are not like the movement of a ship at all: it is as though some vast steel works … were flying unsteadily through the air. Almost as alarming as the movement are the sounds of a battleship in a storm; sounds to which the landsman can give no name and for which he can find no explanation: sudden bumps and bangs of ferocious power, as if the ship had struck a rock or had been kicked by a passing leviathan, followed by an uneasy silence in which metallic objects fall with a crash and men are heard far away running in heavy boots on steel decks.
>
> I lay in electric light with an electric fan turning, trying to read … and I wondered too, how Mr Churchill was getting on on the deck above me.[1]

Mr Churchill was, in fact, very uncomfortable in the Admiral's quarters above and eventually demanded to be taken to the Admiral's sea cabin up on the bridge. In the blacked out ship this was a dangerous move and involved climbing a series of metal ladders, equivalent in height to one of the towers of Westminster Abbey. The young officer escorting the plump sixty-six year old Prime Minister through the darkness worried that the long climb would be too much for him. He worried even more when his torch went out and the two were left to make the climb in total darkness. But Churchill responded scornfully, 'Young man, do you imagine that I have never climbed a ladder in my life?'

The Churchill who set off in that terrible storm to meet the President gave the strong impression of someone on an outing, and very much in holiday mood. The chief purpose of his several journeys to meet with Roosevelt was, of course, the discussion of some crucial, world-historical issues. But another element in these meetings was the pleasure of travelling, of getting away from the daily grind of exercising supreme political power, of having a break, and indeed a good time. For instance Churchill ensured that he and his party ate and drank well on board *Prince of Wales*. Alexander Cadogan of the Foreign Office, Eton and Balliol, brought up by his parents, the Earl and Countess Cadogan amidst the sumptuous hospitality of the imposing Chelsea House in Cadogan Square, was very much a gourmet and his diaries refer repeatedly to the food served on the voyage. He especially enjoyed a dinner of 'good young grouse' that had been put on board in Scotland. (Several dozen grouse were frozen and saved for the President.) At this same dinner Harry Hopkins 'produced a tub of admirable caviar, given him by Joe Stalin'. 'As the PM said it was very good to have such caviar, even though it meant fighting with the Russians to get it.' Churchill enjoyed the food and the wine hugely. And, of course, the long sequence of after dinner brandies. 'When Harry Hopkins refused a second brandy PM said, "I hope that, as we approach the US, you are not going to become more temperate." '

Churchill had also brought films with him for the after dinner entertainment of himself and his friends. His favourite was *Lady Hamilton* with Laurence Olivier and Vivien Leigh, a film which climaxes with the victory and death of Nelson at Trafalgar. When the showing of the film came to an end, Churchill turned to the naval officers in the audience who were veterans of the recent battle with the *Bismarck* and with that throb of emotion about history which was part of his psychological make-up observed, 'I thought this would interest you gentlemen, many of whom have recently engaged with the enemy in matters of equal historical importance'.

The following day was 9 August, the day the *Prince of Wales* was scheduled to anchor close to the heavy cruiser the USS *Augusta* bearing the President of the United States. As this important, dramatic moment approached, Morton noted that as a result of the voyage Churchill was in excellent spirits; 'so much good had the rest done him, that he was not only sprightly but, there is no other word for it, boyish ...'

Morton, a great admirer of Churchill, further particularises this aspect of Churchill's multi-faceted personality which appeared as he prepared to meet the President. 'It is perhaps that part of him which is sensed by crowds in picture theatres, who laugh with delight when they see him waving from the hood of a taxi, or holding his hat on a walking-stick – for Winston has always had a juvenile love for wearing comic hats – and when they observe him twinkling merrily at some parade or pausing wickedly to make that gesture which in England has not always meant V for Victory, they express an appreciation for him which they could never feel for an entirely grown-up, dried-up human being.'[2]

On that last day of the voyage of *Prince of Wales* to its destination, which was now known to be off the coast of the then British colony of Newfoundland, Churchill drilled his British colleagues and crew in all the complex formalities of meeting and greeting which he considered due to the President and, of course, to himself. In these elaborate rehearsals the stiff, aristocratic Cadogan had to stand in, rather self-consciously, for the President.

Whilst these careful, elaborate preparations were being made at sea, in Newfoundland a young American officer in photographic reconnaissance received a radio order to return immediately from his surveying mission to his base at Gander Lake. There he was instructed to pick up the general commanding American forces in Newfoundland and fly him to Argentia Bay, one of the places the Americans now had on lease in return for the aged destroyers they had made available to Britain. As the young officer and his companions flew over the mountains behind Placentia, densely wooded with fir and larch, and looked down into the steel grey waters of the bay, they were astonished at what they saw. Not just one more empty inlet. There amazingly enough, in that remote and desolate place was a vast flotilla of ships, some of them the very big ships of the United States Navy. As the little plane flew down the young officer identified amidst a number of destroyers and smaller vessels the cruiser *Tuscaloosa*, the battle ship *Arkansas* and the heavy cruiser *Augusta*, the flag ship of the Atlantic fleet. He and his companions, he later recalled, flew over this fleet of ships 'frowning with perplexity'. But perhaps he was being a little disingenuous, for being who he was he must have had some inkling of why he had been summoned here. For the officer was Elliott Roosevelt, the thirty-year-old son of the President.

When he and his companions landed, a tender swiftly conveyed them to the *Augusta*. As they were piped aboard Elliott saw several of his father's senior aides standing about on the deck. And then, another surprise, he caught sight of his younger brother, Franklin Roosevelt Junior. Elliott was so taken aback that he forgot an item of naval etiquette that he had been taught years before when his father was Under Secretary of the Navy. Gently reminded, he turned and saluted the United States flag flying at the stern of the cruiser.

The two brothers were then taken to the Captain's quarters. Here they found their father, the Commander-in-Chief looking extremely well, very pleased to see them and, like Churchill, in boyishly good spirits. 'He was as delighted as a kid, boasting of how he had thrown the newspaper men off the scent by going as far as Augusta, Maine, on the presidential yacht *Potomac*.'[3] The press thought he was on a fishing trip. He and Churchill had agreed that there should be no media coverage of their meeting. 'After that, in carrying out his part of the bargain, he enjoyed himself thoroughly, giving the press the slip, much as a twelve-year-old boy playing cops and robbers will enjoy shaking off a playmate who is trying to "shadow" him.'[4]

Then the President grew more serious as he gave to each of his sons an aiguillette, that is to say, an item of military insignia that established each of the brothers as an official aide-de-camp to the Commander-in-Chief. In writing of her husband Eleanor Roosevelt once remarked, 'Perhaps anyone who has not experienced the loneliness of being the President can not appreciate what having a member of the family near one might mean'.[5] Such loneliness, which was something he shared with Churchill and which helped him to bond with him, was a condition which Roosevelt characteristically sought to mitigate by developing personal relations with individuals in politics. And none were more personal than those with his sons whom he made privy to some of the most sensitive and secret issues of the crumbling peace and the coming war.

After they had talked about family news over lunch, the President started to quiz Elliott, who had recently visited London when the Blitz was at its height, about conditions in Britain. As Elliott was speaking of the hardships, the shabbiness but also the endurance of the people, his father asked, 'A meeting like this one will do a world of good for British morale. Won't it?' Elliott agreed. And then his father made it plain that he was fully aware that Churchill was coming to this meeting to seek for more than this. 'Churchill's greatest concern is how soon will we be in the war. He knows very well that so long as the American effort is confined to production, it will do no more than keep England in.'[6] Only if America entered the war, could the Germans be defeated.

Elliott then wondered aloud what there was to gain from this Atlantic meeting. 'Aside, of course, from our being on Britain's side already, morally.' His father replied, 'There's that and it's important'. He said he also wanted 'the exact status of British war potential'. He went on to speak of his admiration for Britain as a democratic force against Nazism but also of his reservations about Britain as also the centre of a huge, repressive and regressive imperial system.

Then Averell Harriman who had been organising Lend Lease at the London end came in, accompanied by Sumner Welles, the rather stiff and punctilious Under

Secretary of State, with whom the President had struck up yet one more personal relationship, in this case, in matters of foreign policy, a relationship that both excluded and greatly irritated Welles's boss the Secretary of State, Cordell Hull.

Some months on the career of Sumner Welles would come to an end as a result of a scandal involving his homosexuality. But Averell Harriman continued as a force in the Democratic Party for over another forty years. As late as the early eighties when he was over ninety he visited the Kremlin to discuss Soviet–American relations. And as a handsome young man in the twenties he could have figured in a novel by Scott Fitzgerald. He had the kind of immense wealth of those around Jay Gatsby and he was part of a glamorous international set such as is described in *Tender Is The Night*. A rowing coach at Yale University Harriman was an expert skier and polo player. His first wife ran a commercial art gallery in Manhattan specialising in the modernist art of the twenties. His second wife, after a failed marriage to Winston Churchill's son Randolph, also pursued a long career in the Democratic Party, and was appointed American Ambassador to Paris by President Bill Clinton. Averell Harriman was from a very different wing of the Democratic Party from that of Harry Hopkins but he like Sumner Welles was one of the most important and influential of this President's men. As Roosevelt waited for Churchill to arrive, he was keen to confer with them one last time about how the meeting should be handled.

Elliott Roosevelt left his father with these close advisers and did not see him again until dinner. The conversation at that meal was mainly small talk. Churchill was clearly very much on the President's mind. He was a little tense about the coming encounter. That night the American party on board the *Augusta* went to bed early.

And they were also up early, that following Saturday morning to see the towering *Prince of Wales* flying a large white ensign slide slowly to its berth and drop anchor not far from the *Augusta*. The contrast between the American vessels and the massive British battleship was striking. *Augusta* and her sister ships from this non-belligerent navy were uncamouflaged and looked smart and sleek in their peacetime grey. These ships from a neutral country had gleaming brass and beautifully maintained pine-white woodwork. *Prince of Wales*, by contrast, looked soiled and tarnished, even a little rusty. The damage done in the *Bismarck* action was still not completely repaired. The large, eerily shabby ship such as might have been captained by the Flying Dutchman fascinated the American sailors who crowded the decks to watch her come to anchor.

Launches from the host ship went alongside carrying less high ranking officers. And then there was a very audible buzz of excitement among the British sailors on the *Prince of Wales* when at eleven o'clock precisely Winston Churchill in the naval cap and blue uniform of the Warden of the Cinque Ports descended into the Admiral's barge and was taken over the narrow strip of grey water to the *Augusta*. The historic meeting was about to begin.

As Churchill came aboard the American ship the marine band saluted him by playing *God Save the King* and after that the *Star Spangled Banner*. Churchill then stepped forward and handed to the President a formal letter of introduction from his head of state, King George VI. The President, wearing a light brown, Palm Beach suit and supported in a standing position by his uniformed son, Elliott Roosevelt, gravely received the letter.

And then suddenly the formalities were relaxed. The

Prime Minister opened his cigar case and the President lit a cigarette. It was a transition that came easily to these gifted politicians. Both enjoyed and studied ceremonial and the semantics of ceremonial. But both were skilled and effective in dealing informally. Yet the first informal exchanges were unfortunate with Churchill tactlessly saying, 'I am happy to meet you at last,' and Roosevelt remembering that occasion in 1918 replying briefly, 'We have met before'. But the pleasantries quickly improved, to the great relief of Harry Hopkins, and then the two leaders went below for cocktails prior to having lunch together. Roosevelt liked to mix strong Martinis made up of dry gin and an especially strong Argentinian vermouth.

Their first conversations were pleasant and light-hearted but there was one matter that had just come to the President's attention and that he raised early on with some urgency and annoyance. And that was the presence on the *Prince of Wales* of British cameramen and of the two writers and journalists, H.V. Morton and Howard Spring, 'the literary gentlemen' as Roosevelt called them. Roosevelt's barely concealed irritation showed up one of the major differences between the President's view of this meeting and Churchill's. To the President the conference at Placentia Bay was just a reconnaissance, a discussion of supply problems and of possible American diplomatic and military initiatives to help Britain without actually entering the war. Churchill saw it, in one respect, as a photo opportunity to illustrate to the world the closeness of Britain and the United States. He and Brendan Bracken wanted images and reporting that would indicate imminent American involvement in the war.

To placate the American press which he had so neatly eluded the President insisted that the two British 'literary gentlemen' publish nothing about the meeting for at least a year. He also sent for American military photographers at the new Placentia base to come to take pictures that could be supplied to the American press. Always mindful of the extent to which his presidency was a construct of the media, Roosevelt invariably handled broadcasters and newspapermen with the utmost care. On this occasion he was quite adamant that since no American newsmen were present the British journalists be excluded from the conference. Churchill quickly concurred with these demands.

This done, the first lunch proceeded in a mood of relaxation. In such informal circumstances they soon began to call each other 'Franklin' and 'Winston'. But when their more formal sessions took place they reverted to 'Mr President' and 'Mr Prime Minister'. As the days went by Roosevelt tended more and more to forget such titles but Churchill in public stuck to them rigorously.

The very sociable first lunch ended at about half past two and the two men parted to consult their advisers in preparation for the large formal dinner for the two delegations to be held in the Captain's saloon on the *Augusta* that evening. Throughout the afternoon members of the two teams of experts moved between the ships with many toings and froings of launches and pipings aboard. Naval ceremonial was incessant. Then in the early evening Churchill in a dinner jacket and his senior military advisers in uniform returned to the American flagship. In this, as in the choice of location for the meeting, the political symbolism was clear. It was Churchill who had come to Roosevelt. The President may well have been, deep down, in awe of Churchill's gifts and of his longevity as a world famous man. But on this night Churchill had come to him to make requests, to make his case and to be judged by Franklin Roosevelt.

Under an awning on deck the President and Prime Minister posed before the popping flashlight cameras of the newly arrived photographers. The host and his chief guests were surrounded by their staff members and the little Scottie dog Fala sat contentedly at the feet of his master, the President. Then the party moved into the large saloon of the ship to dine. The President sat at the head of the large table with the Prime Minister on his right and Cadogan on his left. Also present were Professor Lindemann, Harry Hopkins, Sumner Welles, Averell Harriman and all the British and American staff members, together with the President's recently appointed aide-de-camp, Elliott Roosevelt.

That evening as the dining came to an end, and the brandy circulated continually, and the room filled with the smoke from cigars and cigarettes, and Churchill stood up to speak, Elliott Roosevelt saw his father in a way he had never seen him before. Characteristically the President would dominate whatever company he was in, not so much by what he said, but by his very laid back presence, by what Alexander Cadogan described as his 'great natural charm'. But on this night he was but part of an audience. He merely listened whilst Winston Churchill delivered a bravura performance, in front of this small group of men. The Prime Minister reviewed the causes of the war, its development, the present geo-political situation and the various options available in the future. Churchill, in fact, put on a great rhetorical show for the President and his advisers. He was the after dinner entertainer as well as the supplicant. And his way with the English language was both exhilarating and exotic to the Americans. Churchill held his small audience, Elliott Roosevelt recalled, 'with grand, rolling, periodic sentences, never quite too florid, always ripe and fruity to the point where it seemed you'd be able to take his sentences and squeeze them until the juice ran out'.

The verbal style of the listening Americans was very

different, particularly that of the younger, more irreverent ones. As Churchill orated on, they would occasionally whisper together.

'Match?'

'Thanks.'

'Pass me the water pitcher, huh?'

'Ssshh.'

'Lots of vinegar in him, hmmmm?'

'Yeah – and that ain't all.'[7]

But the President listened carefully to Churchill's rhetorical display which was fired by his impassioned plea for American military intervention in the war. The President's expression was very serious and intent; he doodled on the white tablecloth with a burnt match, he took off his pince-nez and rubbed his eyes. Other listeners wondered what effect this powerful rhetorical display would have upon him. After the chiefs of staff had made more modest statements the President announced that he would be prepared to make joint declaration of political objectives with the British. Such a document would show solidarity with Britain; it should also be framed in such a way as to reassure American isolationists in their reservations about Britain as a class-ridden, undemocratic society with a long term imperialist agenda. Churchill immediately ordered Cadogan to go and prepare a preliminary draft of such a declaration. Thus one of the tangible political achievements of this meeting, the Atlantic Charter, as journalists would later call it, was underway.

The emotion that Churchill had introduced into that after-dinner speech and subsequent informal seminar was greatly intensified on the following Sunday morning when Churchill became the host and received the President on *Prince of Wales* for a morning service. The Prime Minister had most carefully organised the occasion to achieve a direct and powerful effect upon the feelings. On the quarterdeck of *Prince of Wales* the ship's pulpit had been draped with the flags of the United States and Great Britain. The ship's company of *Prince of Wales* and some two hundred and fifty American sailors and marines stood assembled under and around the great guns of the battleship. The band of the Royal Marines formed up in front of the gun turret. The American destroyer *McDougal* came alongside and the President again resting on the arm of Elliott Roosevelt was able, with some difficulty, to step across to the British battleship. The Royal Navy band played the *Star Spangled Banner*. With tense determination but also with obvious pain the President leaning on his son walked the distance along the battle deck to his seat next to Churchill's at the front of that silently respectful assembly of sailors. Just as the service began, Churchill's skilful stage management was suddenly and fortunately enhanced when the grey skies that had covered Placentia for days rolled back and the sun shone brightly down.

After prayers for the King and for the President there were sung the three old, simple rousing hymns that Churchill had chosen. First came 'O God Our Help in Ages Past', then 'Onward Christian Soldiers' and finally 'Eternal Father Strong to Save' which the President had especially requested the night before. For H.V. Morton and for other witnesses of the occasion the sound of hundreds of male voices roaring out over the otherwise silent bay was 'almost intolerable in its emotionalism'. Certainly Churchill himself, always susceptible to strong feelings, and even at times to sentimentality, shed tears as the last hymn was sung. Even the aloof unemotional Cadogan remembered this occasion as 'Very impressive'. And Roosevelt also was profoundly affected. When after lunch on *Prince of Wales* he returned to *Augusta* with Elliott, he burst out trembling with emotion, 'If nothing else had happened while we were here, that would have cemented us. 'Onward Christian Soldiers'. We *are*, and we will go on, with God's help.'

In the more than half century since that Sunday morning Presidents and Prime Ministers have rarely been seen to have been affected by such righteous emotion. But there is no doubt that in the Second World War it was a potent force and nowhere more than in the personal bonding that was now developing between Roosevelt and Churchill during this Atlantic meeting.

That Sunday afternoon while Churchill went ashore in his siren suit and picked a bunch of wild flowers and then returned to the battleship for his customary late afternoon nap, the President worked away with Sumner Welles on a revised draft of the Atlantic Charter. The document was creating some division between the two delegations particularly regarding the matter of continuing British imperial preference after the war. Elsewhere on *Augusta* the military chiefs from both sides discussed animatedly the role of Lease-Lend now that the Russians had entered the war. The British wanted the very minimum diverted from them to the Soviet Union. Some senior American officers, however, took the view that the Russians could make more immediate use of the supplies in the bitter ground war against the Germans. Materials and weapons sent to Britain could for the moment only be stockpiled. Such disagreements started to dissolve the intense feeling of solidarity that had been created in the morning.

The tendency to articulate differences continued that night when Churchill returned to the *Augusta* for dinner. This was a much smaller gathering than that at the great performance occasion of the night before. There were just the President, the Prime Minister, a few aides and Elliott Roosevelt and Franklin Junior. The accuracy of Elliott's account of the disagreements voiced that evening has been called into question. But the division between the leaders expressed in the dialogue reported by this writer certainly existed. Whether or not he used these actual words Roosevelt certainly did believe it was because of British Empire trade agreements that 'the people of India and Africa, of all the colonial Near East and Far East, are still as backward as they are'. And we can readily imagine that with suppressed anger Churchill might well have retorted, 'The trade that has made England great shall continue, and under conditions prescribed by England's ministers'.[8]

But Churchill's anger was, and had to be, suppressed. Even when Roosevelt went on to mention his reservations about British rule in India, a cardinal principle in Churchill's thinking, the Prime Minister, very visibly, controlled himself. Perhaps there are moments in a friendship, even early on in one, when limits have to be tested and when genuine differences have to be expressed, recognised and assimilated by both parties. Perhaps that is a definition of an indispensable and strange feature of the process which is friendship. In any event, controlling his angry impulses towards the man on whose goodwill so much depended, Churchill smoothly changed the subject and managed to bring Harry Hopkins and the Roosevelt sons into the conversation as a way of diffusing the confrontation.

As it turned out the flashes of antagonism between the two men helped confirm the relationship rather than weaken it. When the party broke up and Elliott helped his father to his cabin, the President grunted and said, 'A real old Tory, isn't he? A real old Tory of the old school.' Elliott laughed and said, 'I thought for a minute he was going to bust, Pop.' As they continued to smoke their bedtime cigarettes, the President smiled and said, 'I'll be able to work with him. Don't worry about that. We'll get along famously.'[9]

The following Monday was the last full day of the conference. The morning was given over to further discussions and revisions of the Atlantic Charter. The session also considered Churchill's continuing request that the President take a more menacing line towards the Japanese and their expansionism in the Pacific. Other items of strategic importance were taken up, such as the possibility of Nazism coming closer to the United States with a German occupation of the Portuguese island colonies in the Atlantic. The British also urged on the Americans a stronger line against Vichy France.

After the working lunch Roosevelt took some time out. He wrote a letter in response to the one he had received from King George VI; in it he said, 'It has been a privilege to come to know Mr Churchill in this way and I am very confident that our minds travel together.' To one of his aides that afternoon Roosevelt spoke of Churchill as 'the greatest man in the world'.[10]

Churchill himself at this hour had gone ashore and again clambered up the hills and surveyed the Atlantic base presently being built at Placentia. To one observer Churchill in his one-piece suit with short sleeves and trousers cut off above the knees 'looked like some outsize fat boy, lacking only a toy bucket and spade for his afternoon's romp on the beach'. The infantilism that could sometimes show in Churchill's character then appeared, when, having reached the top of the hill, he rolled down rocks on his companions climbing up below and laughed heartily at their discomfort.

There was still more violent and extensive horseplay on that last night of this all male gathering at Placentia, when the young officers on *Prince of Wales* entertained their American counterparts to a guest night or 'rag'. Played into dinner by the band of the Royal Marines, the American guests who were not allowed alcohol on their own ships were generously wined with their dinner. Then came the port and a few thunderflashes were thrown under the visitors' chairs. There was more port and the band played again. More thunderflashes. To the surprise and then the entertainment of the young Americans a piper marched in with his bagpipes and played for a while. After this, more port. Then the mess president organised the steeple chase which, in its several heats, went backwards and forwards over the furniture for several hours.

Americans present that night were to remember the occasion with deep feeling when they received the news, some four months later, that *Prince of Wales* had been sunk by the Japanese torpedo bombers in the Pacific and that virtually the whole crew, including their hosts of that night, had been lost.

Roosevelt and Churchill spent that last night more quietly. They dined informally with just Harry Hopkins and the Roosevelt sons with them. With the time of parting near there was a mood of kindliness even of familial feeling as the diners talked of the past, of their health, of their relatives and friends. Now as at future meetings Churchill and Roosevelt enjoyed each other's talk. Harry Hopkins took a profound pleasure in the visible fact that his two friends with their great gifts and great egos got on so well together.

The following morning early, the rotund little Lord Beaverbrook, a political associate of Churchill's for more than thirty years huffed and puffed his way on to *Prince of Wales* after a miserable journey from London by plane and train. Churchill immediately informed him that he was to return to Washington with the President and there make ready with the Americans to accompany Harriman to Moscow to discuss matters of supply with Stalin. Beaverbrook at first refused to go, but Churchill exerting his formidable will, insisted. Perhaps the mischievous little Canadian took some pleasure in the title of one of the films he had brought for Churchill's home voyage. Starring Laurel & Hardy it was entitled *Saps at Sea*.

That morning the eight propositions of the final draft of the Atlantic Charter were agreed upon. There was then a last lunch for the two delegations after which Churchill, reporting to the King, wrote, 'I am sure I have established warm and deep personal relations with our great friend'.[11] And later, writing to his son Randolph with whom he was always extremely frank, Churchill declared of the meeting with Roosevelt, 'in the three days when we were continually together I feel we made a deep and intimate contact of friendship'.

The formal, as opposed to the informal farewells between the two men took place in a ceremony on the deck of *Augusta*. Churchill had brought with him some illuminated reproductions of the Longfellow poem 'O Ship of State' which the President had sent him at the height of the Blitz. The copies were signed by both men, the President taking one and the Prime Minister the other. They also exchanged autographed photos of themselves. The cameramen took their pictures as the two men shook hands and the band played. Then Churchill descended into his lauch and left *Augusta* for the last time.

On the stroke of five o'clock that Tuesday afternoon *Prince of Wales* moved slowly out of her berth and set out on the dangerous voyage through the U boats back to Scotland. As the doomed British battleship passed *Augusta* the American band played 'Auld Lang Syne'. In one last rhetorical and emotional gesture Churchill had this final signal sent by flashing light from the departing *Prince of Wales*:

To The President from His Majesty's Government and the British Commonwealth.
God bless the President and People of the United States.
Winston Churchill

Notes

1. H.V. Morton, *Atlantic Meeting* (Methuen, 1943), p. 50.
2. Ibid., pp. 65–66.
3. Elliott Roosevelt, *As He Saw It* (New York, Duell, Sloan & Pearce, 1946), p. 19.
4. Ibid., p. 20.
5. Eleanor Roosevelt in her Introduction to Elliott Roosevelt's *As He Saw It*, p. viii.
6. Elliott Roosevelt, p. 23.
7. Ibid., p. 29.
8. Ibid., p. 36.
9. Ibid., p. 39.
10. Theodore A. Wilson, *The First Summit: Roosevelt and Churchill at Placentia Bay* (Boston, Houghton Mifflin, 1969), p. 167.
11. Ibid., p. 212.

3   Together at Christmas

True friendship is never serene.
Madame de Sévigné

In the immediate aftermath of the Atlantic Conference, as Roosevelt back in America insisted that he had made no commitments to enter the war, there was in Britain a pervasive mood of disappointment, what Churchill himself called 'a wave of depression'. This was something Churchill himself felt very deeply during the last months of 1941. So when Japan attacked the American fleet at Pearl Harbor and America at last entered the war not only against Japan but also against Germany and Italy, Churchill had an overwhelming sense of relief and new hope. In fact the news caused him to have a massive, memorable psychological experience. He would later write of that turning point in the war in virtually religious terms, remembering how 'being saturated and satiated with emotion and sensation, I went to bed and slept the sleep of the saved and the thankful'.[1]

Immediately he wanted to be off to Washington to discuss with Roosevelt the new alliance and the conduct of the war. He would brook no delay in setting off. The President was taken aback by Churchill's haste. He suggested postponing the visit. This was perhaps because he wanted to get his own thoughts and arrangements in order before dealing with the force of Churchill's personality and of his arguments on strategy.

Roosevelt was also worried about Churchill sailing across the U-boat-infested Atlantic directly to Hampton Roads in Virginia as the Prime Minister proposed. Roosevelt urged him to consider travelling via Canada or flying via Bermuda and so avoid the 'great personal risk to you'. The President added in a tone of understanding and admiration, 'I know you will disregard anything I may say to you about the personal risk but I want you to remember that it is essential for the Empire and us that you stay at the helm'.[2]

But Churchill soon had his way. Just two days later he took a train to Gourock on the Clyde where he boarded the battleship HMS *Duke of York*. This was the sister ship to the *Prince of Wales* which, to Churchill's great grief, had been sunk by the Japanese off Singapore just three days before. The voyage to the coast of Virginia took ten days. And for the first week or so the gales were heavy and incessant. Churchill, never a good sailor, recalled in an affectionate letter to his wife Dr Johnson's statement that 'No man will be a sailor who has contrivance enough to get himself into jail; for being in a ship is being in a jail with the chance of being drowned'.

But he went on to say that with 'tremendous seas pouring over the bows of the ship' he had nevertheless been able to work on position papers to do with aspects of the larger strategy of the war. Fretting about the length of the voyage the amateur painter conceded that 'it is perhaps a good thing to stand away from the canvas from time to time and take a full view of the picture'. The papers on strategy constituting 'the full view' were thrust upon the Americans almost immediately after Churchill and his small party had disembarked.

After HMS *Duke of York* had docked Churchill flew on to Washington where the President sat awaiting him in his personal car. The warmth of feeling between the two men at this moment was suggested by Churchill in the simple sentence with which he began his account of this second wartime meeting: 'I clasped his strong hand with comfort and pleasure'.[3] And such feeling persisted throughout the three weeks that Churchill now spent in the United States. As a guest at the White House Churchill was closer to Roosevelt than he had been at Argentia. Henry Hopkins recalled the ready, happy intimacy that developed between them at this time. But it was always contained within the decorum appropriate to the dealings of a head of state with a head of government. Churchill with his Tory insistence upon hierarchy always bore this in mind. After their meals together he got into the habit of 'wheeling the handicapped President from the dining room to the lift'. This Churchill did, he said, 'as a mark of respect'.

At this Christmas time in Washington the two men related to each other as public figures as well as private individuals. Americans were still in shock after Pearl Harbor and the worldwide war in which they suddenly found themselves. They were keen to see and to know more about their new ally. Early on in his stay Churchill accompanied President Roosevelt to a White House press conference and quickly established a good relationship with the American journalists and radio broadcasters. Just as he could entertain the President so he entertained them. He said quotable things, he mocked Hitler and Mussolini; he made jokes. When the President indicated to him that the pressmen at the back of the room could not see him properly, he stood up. When this was not enough, America's new ally and hero climbed up confidently and stood on his chair. This helpful gesture brought a good deal of appreciative applause and cheering.

On Christmas Eve Churchill enjoyed another enthusiastic reception when he stood beside the President on a balcony and watched the lights of the huge White House Christmas tree come on. Thousands and thousands of people, some inside, some outside the grounds of the White House listened as Churchill spoke to them very personally of his feeling of being at home in the United States. 'Whether it be the ties of blood on my mother's side, or the friendships I have developed over many years of active life … I cannot feel myself a stranger here in the centre and at the summit of the United States. I feel a sense of unity and fraternal association …'[4] Similar sentiments informed Churchill's speech to a joint session of Congress on the day after Christmas. The senators and congressmen laughed a good deal at his statement, 'if my father had been an American and my mother British, instead of the other way around, I might have got here on my own'. But what they really wanted, as they set about facing the realities of war, was one of his rousing orations. And this, to Roosevelt's delight, he gave them. His resounding speech in which he asserted his confidence both in the new alliance and in its ultimate victory brought the entire Congress to its feet in a wildly enthusiastic ovation that lasted until Churchill left the chamber of the House. The friendship between Roosevelt and Churchill which so intensified during these weeks was in great part enhanced by the strong public admiration which these two very political men enjoyed together and involved each other in.

But along with these efforts in public relations so much appreciated and reported and photographed by the media there was also a good deal of hard work done at this Washington meeting. During the three weeks the two delegations met more than a dozen times to discuss difficult issues of supply and command within the new alliance. Churchill, unlike Roosevelt always involved himself in all the fine details of these matters. More than two years of such hard work took its toll and it was at this time, on Boxing Day 1941, whilst Churchill was struggling to open a window in his bedroom at the White House that he first experienced that acute heart pain which Lord Moran, the doctor who from now on would always accompany Churchill, diagnosed as 'coronary insufficiency'. The world was not to know until after the two men were dead the extent to which the leaders of the wartime alliance were sick men. Churchill worried privately about his heart condition; Roosevelt was beginning to be, at times, incapacitated by diastolic hypertension and by iron deficiency due to bleeding haemorrhoids. Small wonder that health was often a topic of conversation between these two men now both in their sixties. But they always spoke of it fatalistically, jokingly.

And joking became a part of this holiday time meeting. The relationship, increasingly less formal than at Argentia, had become relaxed enough for that. At the Christmas Eve dinner at the White House Roosevelt teased Churchill at some length about having been on the wrong side in the Boer War at the turn of the century. In the first of the rebellions in this century against Britain's world wide imperial system, the Afrikaaners had enjoyed the enthusiastic support of the teenage Franklin Roosevelt. Forty years on he now joked about Churchill's credentials as a champion of democracy, given the attitude to the Boer rebellion he had expressed in his book about the war, *London to Ladysmith via Pretoria*. But Churchill, ever the unhesitating imperialist, hit back with sentences of Johnsonian trenchancy and wit, one of the sentences containing a subordinate clause about America's role in the Philippines. But soon he turned the conversation round to what he regarded as the excessive amounts of powdered egg in the food supply America was sending to Britain. As one who was impressed by the invention and the potential of powdered egg Roosevelt was irritated and a little hurt when Churchill, steadily sipping his brandy, continued to insist that it was only usable in puddings. 'Nonsense,' snapped Roosevelt. 'You can do as much with a powdered egg as a real egg. 'No, no,' persisted Churchill, 'the only thing you can make with them is Spotted Dick'.

At the White House lunch on New Year's Day differences between the Americans and the British on matters of lifestyle were again the source of humour. This time the subject was personal hygiene. Churchill who remembered the old 'rub down' in his days as a young cavalry officer on the Indian frontier with Afghanistan, now launched into a denunciation of showers and bathtubs. He couldn't understand, he declared innocently, why there was so much enthusiasm for 'these newfangled Ba-a-athtubs'. They were an American contrivance that had been foisted on the British. But when challenged by the President, Churchill who liked to play the part of the old unwashed Tory, especially for Americans, finally conceded that he had enjoyed a hot bath before this very meal, 'lying back and kicking one's legs in the air as at birth'. A little earlier in the visit after enjoying another such bath in the White House Churchill in his bathrobe had moved into his adjacent bedroom and study, all the time dictating to one of his secretaries, Patrick Kinna. The bathrobe fell off but Churchill continued to dictate. Suddenly President Roosevelt in his wheelchair was brought into the room. But the naked Churchill was unperturbed. In a remark that contained a snipe at those Americans such as General 'Vinegar' Joe Stilwell, who worried about British self-interest and duplicity, Churchill observed, 'You see, Mr President, I have nothing to conceal from you'. Reporting back to England from the White House, Churchill wrote, 'We live here as a big family in the greatest intimacy and informality ...'[5]

But for all the relaxed atmosphere and the jokes Churchill who knew himself to be the dependent one in the relationship showed great tact in not going too far. For example his five-day trip to Florida during his stay was undertaken, according to Lord Moran, so that he would not run the risk of outstaying his welcome at the White House. But there was also thoughtfulness from the other side. Roosevelt, who did not know at this time of Churchill's cardiac difficulties in Washington, neverthe-less thought that the Prime Minister looked extremely tired after all his exertions and urged him to take the vacation in the sun.

The sheer hard work of the two put in at these Washington meetings produced some considerable achievement. When Churchill came to leave, he and President Roosevelt had developed a great sense of unity of purpose and important logistical arrangements had been agreed on. Their unity was expressed in a document which was an extension and elaboration of the Atlantic Charter. At first the new statement was called the Allied Declaration of Unity and Purpose. But when it was read out that New Year's Day of 1942, Churchill agreed with Roosevelt that the aims of all those countries resisting the Axis powers should be abbreviated to the Declaration of the United Nations. And so originated a phrase and a document that led finally to a charter and an institution that were to be an important political entity in the post-war world.

Churchill, the man of letters, who in the worst storms at sea would recall the words of Samuel Johnson, now recalled, much to the President's interest, that the phrase United Nations appeared in the poetry of that other freedom fighter, Lord Byron. To the assembled guests at that White House dinner Churchill recited the stanza from *Childe Harold's Pilgrimage.*

> Here, where the sword United Nations drew,
> Our countrymen were warring on that day
> All this is much – and all – which will not pass away.

After Roosevelt and Churchill had signed the declaration, Maxim Litvinov, the Washington Ambassador of the Soviet Union signed on behalf of his country. Subsequently the document was signed by the representatives of twenty-three other countries some of which were under Nazi occupation. For Roosevelt and Churchill the public occasion always alternated with the private one. Theirs was a relationship founded on more than political business. And after the public signing of the statement expressing the principles of the United Nations, Churchill in the President's office signed two of his books which the President owned. In a volume of his speeches he wrote, 'Inscribed by Winston S. Churchill, January 1, 1942 at the moment of signing the Declaration of United Nations'. The other book from Roosevelt's personal library was the first volume of Churchill's *The River War* published just over forty years earlier in 1900. It was the young writer's first hand account of the British expedition down the Nile to re-establish British power in the Sudan after the Islamic fundamentalist uprisings towards the end of the nineteenth century at which time General Gordon had met his death. Inside this book dating from the zenith of British imperial confidence Churchill now wrote, in the aftermath of Dunkirk and Pearl Harbor, 'Inscribed for President Franklin Roosevelt by Winston Churchill. In rough times January 1942'.[6]

As the time for Churchill's departure neared, Roosevelt again grew anxious about his friend's safety on the Atlantic on board the *Duke of York*. He urged him to accept the use of an American aircraft, a Boeing Clipper, a large passenger flying boat that had been developed at Seattle in the late 1930s. Churchill was less concerned about his safety than about the amount of time the sea voyage would take. He did not want to be away from his political control centre in London for another ten days as on the voyage out. So he finally accepted the President's offer and went aboard the Clipper where it rode at anchor at Norfolk, Virginia. It was, General Brooke, one of Churchill's military advisers, was to remember, a striking example of pre-war luxury air travel; a 'Huge flying boat, beautifully fitted up with bunks to sleep in, dining room, steward's office, lavatories etc.' Another senior British officer, plump Pug Ismay, luxuriated in the 'easy chairs and the delicious food'.

It took some eighteen hours before the large, silver, gleaming flying boat touched down in English waters near Plymouth Hoe. During the flight Churchill made it plain to the American captain that he would like to take control of the aircraft. He piloted it for some twenty minutes, even attempting one or two banked turns. When he stepped ashore in bomb blackened Plymouth Churchill's morale was excellent. The political alliance and the personal friendship were alike mounting. His farewell with the President had been not so much ceremonial or formal as emotional. Over their parting handshake the President had said, earnestly, slowly and emphatically. 'Trust me to the bitter end'.[7]

The visit to the President in Washington brought immense reassurance to Churchill. After nearly two years of setback and defeat, he felt new promise and new hope. But this happy optimism was to prove short-lived. Within just days of his return to London he was to become deeply disheartened and, with Roosevelt looking on helplessly, to experience the first great psychological crisis of his premiership.

Notes

1. Winston S. Churchill, *The Second World War*, 6 Vols (Cassell, 1948–53), *The Grand Alliance*, p. 243.
2. Kimball, p. 286.
3. Churchill, p. 294.
4. Martin S. Gilbert, *Winston Churchill: Road To Victory* (Heineman, 1986), p. 27.
5. Ibid., p. 36.
6. Kimball, p. 310.
7. Gilbert, p. 43.

4 A Friend in Need

We cannot tell the precise moment when friendship is formed.
As in filling a vessel drop by drop, there is a last drop which
makes it run over; so in a series of kindnesses there is at least
one which makes the heart run over.
James Boswell, *Life of Johnson*, September 1777

After his eighteen hour flight to Plymouth over the wintry
North Atlantic the sixty-seven-year-old Churchill
developed a very heavy cold. Anthony Eden, the Foreign
Secretary, found him 'tired and depressed' as they
prepared to face a vote of confidence in the House of
Commons. After this had been won, with only one vote
against, Churchill went out to an evening party and tried
to dance but had to give up when his heart beat violently
and he lost his breath.

His morale was further weakened by the so-called
'Channel Dash', the incident in which three German
warships, *Gneisenau, Scharnhorst* and *Prinz Eugen* left the
port of Brest in Brittany and managed to sail through the
twenty-one-mile narrows of the Straits of Dover and
thence return to safety in Germany. The failure of the
Royal Navy and the Air Force to prevent this daring
escape caused much criticism of the government in the
press. But worse, far worse was to come. Two days later
Britain's great Pacific fortress and naval harbour,

Singapore, capitulated to the Japanese. Eighty thousand British and allied soldiers surrendered.

To Churchill the loss of this major component in the system of British worldwide imperial power was traumatic. He described it as 'the worst disaster and largest capitulation in British history'. And writing to Roosevelt about the effects of this disaster in the Pacific, Averell Harriman, who was continuing to 'facilitate' Lease Lend, reported from London that it had robbed Churchill of 'his old vigour'. The ignominious surrender at Singapore had shaken him and tired him. And around this same time Cadogan observed the 'Poor old PM in a sour mood and a bad way'.

At this painful time in Churchill's life Roosevelt was not slow to take up one of the responsibilities of friendship, the expression of every possible support and sympathy. In this he had the help of the new American Ambassador in London, John Gilbert Winant, a ladies' man and an Abraham Lincoln look-alike who reminded the President that 'a cheery word from you and Harry always lightens his load'. In an extended telegram Roosevelt told Churchill, 'I realise how the fall of Singapore has affected you and the British people'. He went on in a more personal tone, 'I hope you will be of good heart in these trying weeks because I am very sure that you have the great confidence of the masses of the British people'. Still more sympathetically he continued, 'I want you to know that I think of you often and I know you will not hesitate to ask me if there is anything you think I can do'.[1]

Churchill was quick to send his thanks for 'your warm hearted telegram'. He admitted that he did 'not like these days of personal stress and I have found it difficult to keep my eye on the ball'. But he was anxious to make it clear to the President that he was in no way faltering or unreliable. 'You may take it everything is now solid.'

But a month later, in mid March of 1942, Roosevelt was still expressing concern about his friend's situation. This time he wrote him a long and at times very personal letter which began, 'I am sure you know that I have been thinking about your troubles during the past month'. The President then proceeded to offer thoughts and kindly advice about certain war matters. On occasion he adopts the tone of the patrician and imperial President when he speaks of the inadequacies of 'My Navy'. But the letter concludes with a paragraph of very warm and human fellow-feeling. Roosevelt writes, 'I know you will keep up your optimism and your grand driving force, but I know you will not mind if I tell you that you ought to take a leaf out of my notebook. Once a month I go to Hyde Park for four days, crawl into a hole and pull the hole in after me. I am called on the telephone only if something of really great importance occurs. I wish you would try it, and I wish you would lay a few bricks or paint another picture'. The letter ends with the hope that their wives may become involved in the friendship. 'Give my warm regards to Mrs Churchill. I wish much that my wife and I could see her.'[2]

Churchill was greatly heartened by this very personal statement of concern and good will. He soon replied, 'Delighted by your letter of March eighteenth just received. I am so grateful to you for all your thoughts about my affairs and personal kindness'. He responded warmly to the President's allusion to their wives and took advantage of this moment of explicit closeness to suggest another visit to Washington. 'Perhaps when the weather gets better I may propose myself for a weekend with you and flip over'.

These verbal exchanges of friendship were accompanied by small but significant tokens and gifts. In early May Roosevelt sent Churchill an envelope with a stamp that had been franked on his flagship *Augusta* at the time of their meeting off Newfoundland. The President wrote, 'I found this envelope among my things yesterday. Even if you prefer the trade of bricklaying to the great science of philately, you may have a descendant who collects stamps. I think it was postmarked on the *Augusta* at the moment you stepped over the side'. Churchill soon reciprocated. 'I am venturing to send you a collection of the books I have written, which I have had bound up, hoping you will find a place for them in your shelves.' Roosevelt duly replied, 'I am thrilled at the thought of the books and shall always cherish them'. The volumes arrived in Washington just a week before Churchill flew over for his third conference with the President. On that very day on which Roosevelt received Churchill's gift the British Eighth Army in its struggle against Rommel west of the North African port of Tobruk suffered a massive setback. By midday it had lost a hundred and thirty tanks. By nightfall only seventy-five remained operational. The remnants of the British army fell back towards the fortress of Tobruk in total disarray.

In the War Cabinet in London there was some uneasiness about the Prime Minister leaving the country with such a crisis developing in the fight for the coast of North Africa and the Mediterranean. But Churchill had urgent concerns on his mind which, he was sure, could only be dealt with in face to face conversations with the President. He was, for instance, extremely worried about the American determination to mount an invasion of Europe before the end of 1942. Just a few months earlier Harry Hopkins and General Marshall had been sent to London to explain the plan to Churchill. And Roosevelt himself told Churchill, enthusiastically, that what his two emissaries were coming to put before him, 'has my heart and mind in it'. But Churchill had serious doubts about the success of such an invasion. He also realised that failure to initiate some definite and dramatic action against the Germans might allow American opinion to move away from the commitment to a 'Germany First' policy. The American victory at the great aircraft carrier battle at Midway which had halted the rapid Japanese expansion in the Pacific greatly encouraged those Americans who questioned whether the war against Japan should be their country's secondary enterprise. Churchill was anxious to resist the influence of such an idea, especially on the mind of the President.

Another urgent matter for Churchill was the programme then codenamed Tube Alloys. This was the research which would ultimately lead to the manufacture of an atomic bomb. Both Britain and America had invested in this research which had developed at such a pace that it was now necessary to co-ordinate the programmes and to decide where production facilities should be built. The matter needed immediate attention for it was now known that the Germans were also endeavouring to develop atomic weaponry.

So despite the crisis of the thirty-two thousand British soldiers now besieged in Tobruk and the rest of the British army retreating pell mell into Egypt, Churchill felt that he had to leave London to have his say with the President. Above all he wanted to argue for operation TORCH, American landings in Morocco and Algeria which would link up with the British campaign in North Africa. On this Churchill had set his mind. On June 17th he travelled in his special train from Euston up to Stranraer in south western Scotland where he was to board the Boeing Clipper which at his insistence the British government had now acquired. Churchill took with him members of his personal staff including his valet and his doctor, Lord Moran. Churchill was also accompanied by his two senior military advisers. One was Hastings Ismay known as Pug because he looked like one. He was a plump, portly down to earth army officer who was Churchill's chief of staff in relation to the Ministry of Defence. The other professional adviser who set off with Churchill from Stranraer on this trip to Washington was General Alan Brooke whom Churchill had made chief of Britain's Imperial General Staff.

Brooke was from one of the aristocratic families of Northern Ireland. In his late fifties at this time he was a distinguished looking man with a greying moustache, receding hair and large intelligent eyes. He had great charm and was a suave administrator. He was intrigued to think that such an important episode in the history of the war and the world should begin in the quiet little harbour of Stranraer. Looking out on to the glinting, still waters of Loch Ryan he could see the silver Clipper at anchor, shining in the gentle pink of that summer dusk. To the north in the distance loomed the dark mass of the Mull of Kintyre.

The little party of powerful men walked down the quay in this quiet place, so remote from all the dramas of the world war. Churchill himself was an improbable, slightly comic figure. He was, Brooke remembered, 'dressed in his zip-suit and zip shoes with a black Homburg hat on the side of his head and his small gold-tipped malacca cane in his hand'. Clearly Churchill shared Brooke's sense of the strangeness of the place and the situation in which they here found themselves for the Prime Minister started to sing one of the absurdist songs of the First World War. 'Suddenly almost like Pooh-Bear, he started humming, "We are here because we're here – We're here because we're here".' For Brooke the choice of song was perfectly appropriate because this was 'a time when the Atlantic had not been so very frequently flown' and 'we were both somewhat doubtful why we were going, whether we should get there, what we should achieve while we were there, and whether we should ever get back'.[3]

But after this peculiar moment or two of hesitation and contemplation the party stepped down into the motor boat and was ferried out to the Clipper.

The flight was an enjoyable one, much more so than many of the later ones Churchill was to undertake to meet the President. The meals were excellent and all washed down with champagne and brandy. The travellers looked down on the Irish coast. They visited the pilot on what Brooke called 'his driving-compartment on top bridge.' They flew over a convoy of thirty-five ships. They admired the light of the full moon on the clouds. They saw 'wonderful red sky from just below the horizon ... the silver wings of the clipper reflecting this glorious colour'. They had a long morning in bed before their late and large breakfast in the aircraft's dining room. They flew over Gander in Newfoundland to have a view of the new airport and then headed south over New England and on to Washington. As they came into land on the Potomac River Churchill noticed that the immense aircraft was at the same height as, and very close to, the Washington Monument. Only half jokingly he impressed upon Captain Kelly Rogers that it would be 'peculiarly unfortunate if we brought our story to an end by hitting this of all other objects in the world'. But they landed safely and smoothly on a very hot, sticky evening in Washington; they had been flying for just about twenty-seven hours.

Churchill stayed ovenight at the British Embassy. The following morning he flew on to Hyde Park, the family home and estate of the Roosevelts on the high bluffs over the Hudson River some miles to the north of New York City. This very special invitation from the President for

Churchill to visit him at his private residence was, in part, politically motivated; it enabled the two leaders to confer, one to one, before considering all the important matters at issue, particularly the proposed TORCH operation, in the presence of their advisers. But the invitation to Hyde Park also had more personal implications for the two men. It was a clear sign of a further degree of intimacy in the friendship between them.

The airfield closest to Roosevelt's home was Hackensack and here the President waited in his car to welcome his visitor after his flight in a US navy plane over Philadelphia and the skyscrapers of New York City. 'He welcomed me with great cordiality,' Churchill remembered. And then the President took his guest on a tour of his extensive estate in his specially fitted up car. Because of the weakness of his legs there could be no ordinary brake, clutch or accelerator on the automobile the President drove himself. All these devices were so arranged that he could operate them with his hands. His reliance on his arms, Roosevelt pointed out proudly, made them extremely strong and muscular. In an impulse of almost boyish pleasure and triumph the sixty year old President invited Churchill to feel his biceps remarking a little boastfully that a famous boxer had envied them.[4]

He drove his special car, a blue Ford, with every confidence and took great pleasure in showing his visitor the splendid river views. On several occasions when Roosevelt backed the car, fast, on to the grass verges of the precipices over the Hudson River, Churchill grew anxious lest the specially installed mechanical devices might prove to have defects. But for all the hair-raising moments during this drive, the two men talked important business throughout. And, Churchill later recalled, 'though I was careful not to take his attention off the driving, we made more progress than we might have done in formal conference'.

An important topic for discussion on that beautiful summer morning was the TORCH operation, Churchill's proposal that the necessary Allied initiative in the war take place in North West Africa rather than in Europe. This was something which the two continued to discuss late into the night as they sped south to Washington in the President's special train. At the White House Churchill was given the same large, air conditioned room he had had on his previous visit at Christmas. When he woke up the following morning he was to receive a piece of news which had a near traumatic effect upon him. This news disrupted utterly the proposed agenda for the conference between the British and American delegations. But it also brought about a dramatic increase of feeling, closeness and sympathy between Winston Churchill and Franklin Roosevelt.

After breakfasting the Prime Minister, together with Alan Brooke, Pug Ismay and Harry Hopkins had gone to the President's study. They were just settling down to a formal session of talk when a presidential aide entered the room and placed a strip of pink paper in the President's hands. It was a wire message. Roosevelt studied it briefly and, without saying a word, passed it to Churchill. The Prime Minister read 'Tobruk has surrendered and twenty-five thousand men taken prisoner'. It did not contain the other devastating piece of news that at Tobruk the Germans had also captured sufficient military supplies and ammunition to enable them to continue fighting for three months more without relying on materials flown out, at considerable danger, from Italy to North Africa. That brief message in Churchill's hands announced one of the major British routs of the war. It was another Singapore. And the Prime Minister felt a sudden, intense shame. 'It was a bitter moment,' he later wrote. 'Defeat is one thing; disgrace is another.'[5]

Onlookers in the President's room that morning could see that Churchill was visibly shaken by the news. In wild disbelief he turned to Pug Ismay and asked him to go and telephone London for confirmation. A few minutes later a solemn, tense Pug Ismay returned with further corroborating information. Churchill sat slumped in his chair. 'I did not attempt to hide from the President the shock I had received,' he recalled later on.

For a while there was silence among the half dozen or so men around the desk in the President's study. And then came a memorable moment in the history of the relationship between Roosevelt and Churchill. The President broke the silence and asked quite simply, 'What can we do to help?'[6]

Churchill looked up, his blurred eyes suddenly shining. The emotions of gratitude swiftly inspired a renewed sense of possibility, purpose and retaliation. He answered urgently, 'Give us as many Sherman tanks as you can spare and ship them to the Middle East as quickly as possible'. Roosevelt nodded and sent immediately for General Marshall who, despite the losses and the setbacks this request would mean for the US Army, readily accepted the President's order to assist Churchill in this terrible hour of calamity.

This act of Roosevelt's was one of those swift impulses of sympathy and generosity which make for friendships. It was an act in excess of, even unhelpful to, what American interests required. But it was a generosity that would stay in Churchill's mind as a potent memory. Amidst later disagreements and irritations that Tobruk morning would be a recollection that would serve to stabilise the friendship.

Of this dramatic moment that very practical, down to

earth soldier, Pug Ismay, who was there in the President's office, has written, 'It was at moments like this that one realised what a priceless asset the Allies possessed in the intimate friendship and mutual understanding between Churchill and Roosevelt. Any mistrust which may have been in those early days between the British and American Chiefs of Staff did not extend to their political masters.'[7] Ismay also speculates about what would have happened if the British request for Sherman tanks had been handled 'through normal official channels'. All he could imagine was a long drawn out process, which if it had produced this American aid at all, would have involved protracted and bureaucratic procedures and a great waste of time. One practical consequence of the Roosevelt–Churchill relationship was that the assistance could be arranged within minutes. For Ismay, formerly an officer in India, now on his first visit to the White House, it had been 'intensely interesting to see Roosevelt and Churchill together at close quarters. There was something so intimate in their friendship. They used to stroll in and out of each other's rooms in the White House, as two subalterns occupying adjacent quarters might have done. Both of them had the spirit of eternal youth. Both were the spokesmen of democracy. Both had superlative courage.'[8]

Churchill would need his courage soon enough. For after a long day of negotiation with the Americans on the several difficult issues facing the alliance and then a brief sleep he woke up to find the headlines in the American newspapers announcing the anger against himself in Britain following the fall of Tobruk: 'CHURCHILL TO BE CENSURED – TOBRUK MAY BRING CHANGE OF GOVERNMENT'.

Churchill refused to be stampeded but he did drastically curtail his stay in Washington in order to return to Westminster and confront his critics. He kept his promise to go and watch American troops training at Fort Jackson, North Carolina. But then he quickly returned to the White House where the President bade him goodbye with, as Churchill remembered, 'all his grace and courtesy'.

The President directed Averell Harriman and Harry Hopkins to see the Prime Minister off. There was a special warmth amongt these men in these last moments in the President's office. For Harry Hopkins had told them not long before that he had become engaged to be married. His fiancée was Mrs Louise Macy who had been a fashion journalist in Paris and who, through mutual friends, had been referred to him for a job in the American war effort. Both Roosevelt and Churchill were delighted for him. And the President, without very extensive consultation with his wife, was quick to inform the bride-to-be that she could and should come to live with Harry in the White House. Thus it was that some six weeks later the government of the United States became centred on what was in some respects a *ménage à quatre*. For Roosevelt the conducting of friendships was always easier and more straightforward than familial arrangements.

Churchill's second trip to Washington ended with Harry Hopkins driving him to Baltimore where the Boeing Clipper awaited him offshore. Over his final handshake with Harry, Churchill said, 'Now for England, home and – a beautiful row'.

The shining aircraft flew off into the night and in the dawn landed at the quiet little harbour of Botwood in Newfoundland in order to refuel. Here Churchill, ever the trencherman, ate a large breakfast of beautiful fresh lobsters well washed down with drink. In the thin light of early morning the Clipper took off again and, twenty-four hours later, glided down on to the waters of the Clyde.

Roosevelt supported by his son Elliott is welcomed aboard
HMS *Prince of Wales* by Churchill

Roosevelt and Churchill at Sunday morning service on *Prince of Wales*
in Placentia Bay, Newfoundland

In a relaxed mood together after the service

Churchill watching the destroyer USS *McDougal* bearing the President away from their final meeting at Placentia Bay

Churchill in the gardens of the White House with Harry Hopkins, his daughter Deana Hopkins and her pet dog. In the centre is Commander Thompson, Churchill's aide-de-camp

Roosevelt with cigarette holder drives Churchill with cigar in his specially equipped car. In the back are Brendan Bracken in spectacles and Commander Thompson

Resting in the rose garden after long discussions in the White House

A confidential moment at Casablanca

At the end of the Casablanca Conference Roosevelt maintains a straight face and Churchill almost does so, as the bride (de Gaulle) and the bridegroom (Giraud) are compelled to be photographed together

Roosevelt with Generalissimo Chiang-Kai-shek in Cairo, 1943. Churchill deplored his influence on the President

The chief photo opportunity at the Cairo Conference. Churchill and
Madame Chiang-Kai-shek conceal their animosities

Churchill convalescing in North Africa at Christmas 1943 is visited by
Generals Eisenhower and Alexander

Canadian Prime Minister Mackenzie King listens to an exchange between Prime Minister Churchill and President Roosevelt on the Citadel in Quebec City

Churchill's sixty-ninth birthday party at Teheran, 1943. On Stalin's left sits the interpreter on whom the dessert was later spilled

Then, turning from the vast, bright summer skies of the North Atlantic Churchill travelled down to a dark, shabby bomb-scarred London where he faced the strongest parliamentary challenge to his leadership since he had become Prime Minister some two years before.

Back in Washington Roosevelt and Harry Hopkins waited in hope and suspense.

Notes

1. Kimball, p. 363.
2. Ibid., pp. 420–422.
3. Arthur Bryant, *The Turn of the Tide* (New York, Doubleday, 1957), p. 322.
4. Gilbert, p. 127.
5. Ibid., p. 128.
6. Winston S. Churchill, *The Second World War, Vol IV*, p. 344.
7. General Lord Ismay, *The Memoirs of General Lord Ismay* (New York, Viking, 1960), p. 255.
8. Ibid., p. 256.

5   Counsels and Contemplations

I want someone to laugh with me, someone to be grave with me, someone to please me and help my discrimination with his or her own remark, and at times, no doubt, to admire my acuteness and penetration.

Robert Burns, Commonplace Book, 9 April 1787

On the first day of July 1942 when the Vote of Censure was moved against Churchill's government in the House of Commons, the news of two more disasters for the Allied cause came in. The Germans had captured the fortress harbour of Sebastapol in the Crimea and Rommel's army had pushed swiftly and dramatically into Egypt and was now less than forty miles from the city of Alexandria.

The House was, therefore, in a mood to listen to the proposer of the censure motion, the Conservative MP Sir John Wardlaw Milne. At the beginning of his speech he compelled attention from all sides as he argued that Churchill was a very amateur strategist, that he meddled disastrously in military matters and that someone more competent should direct the war. But then Wardlaw Milne made the mistake of naming a possible Commander in Chief. He proposed the Duke of Gloucester, the brother of King George VI. Now the plump Duke was far from being renowned for his mental powers and the House rocked with laughter at the suggestion. The speech then sputtered, faltered to a conclusion and at the end of the two day debate the motion was supported by only twenty five MPs with four hundred and seventy five voting in support of the Churchill government. It was a decisive victory but not as decisive as in the previous confidence motion when there had been but one single vote against the government. Also there had been a powerful speech against Churchill's leadership from the fiery, eloquent Welsh MP, Aneurin Bevan, who claimed that the army was 'badly led' and that it was 'ridden by class prejudice'. The left wing Labour member from the Rhondda Valley went on to question Churchill's personal competence. The Prime Minister, he declared ringingly, 'wins debate after debate and loses battle after battle. The country is beginning to say that he fights debates like a war and the war like a debate.'[1]

Nevertheless Churchill had won this debate handsomely and his government was secure. Roosevelt cabled immediately, 'Good for you'. And surely Harry Hopkins was speaking as much for the President as for himself when he telegraphed, 'Action of House of Commons today delighted me. These have been some of the bad days. No doubt there will be others ... I know you are of good heart, for your military defeats and ours, and our certain victories to come, will be shared together. More power to you.'[2] Touched by this strong support from Washington Churchill replied, 'Thank you so much, my friend. I knew you and the President would be glad of this domestic victory'.

In the July weeks that followed his parliamentary success Churchill quickly took energetic steps to deal with the setbacks in both Egypt and Russia. He would himself fly to Cairo to reorganise the military command there. And then he would fly on to Moscow where he would attempt to reassure Stalin about British and American intentions. He knew that Stalin expected much larger supplies to be sent by Arctic convoys to the ports of northern Russia. The Russian leader also demanded that a second front be established in western Europe in order to take the pressure off his armies in the east. Churchill knew that he had to tell Stalin that this was logistically impossible in the near future. But he also wanted to reach an understanding with Stalin, to keep him in the war and to prevent the Soviet Union from concluding a separate peace with Hitler.

On the first day of August Churchill travelled down to RAF Lyneham in Wiltshire where late on a very dark night his wife Clementine saw him off on the first stage of his long journey. This time he could not travel on the luxurious Boeing Clipper but instead flew on a four engined bomber, an American Liberator, bearing the name *Commander*. Clementine later told her husband that 'It was both dramatic and mysterious standing in the dark on that aerodrome while your monster bomber throbbing, roaring and flashing blue light taxied away into the blackness'. Inside the plane there was no heating and no beds. For sleeping there were just mattresses on two shelves built into the sides of the plane. Churchill took one, and his worried doctor, Lord Moran, the other. As Churchill's daughter Mary noted, his 'coronary thrombosis ... might be brought on by anything like a long and/or high flight'. And Moran, his doctor, fretted to see that Churchill was restless and uncomfortable in the chilly Liberator. 'And after all,' wrote Moran in his diary, 'it is a rather feckless way of sending him over the world when he is approaching his seventieth year.'[3]

Yet Churchill arrived in Cairo 'in great heart', taking intense pleasure in being 'the man on the spot', where action was urgently needed. He moved swiftly to make changes in the senior British command structure in Egypt, changes which included the brisk, energetic, General Bernard Montgomery taking over the Eighth Army. Less than three months later Churchill's drastic redeployment of his generals would be vindicated by Britain's first land victory against the Germans in this war, the defeat and dispersal of Rommel's army at El Alamein.

His senior personnel changes completed in Cairo, Churchill flew on in the second week of August to his next difficult mission, his meeting with Stalin in Moscow. He was somewhat apprehensive about this encounter with what Clementine called 'the Ogre in his Den' and he confided his uneasiness to Roosevelt. He very much wanted Stalin to realise that Britain and the United States were at one in strategic policy and he asked Roosevelt if he would allow Averell Harriman, who had proved himself a skilful Lend Lease administrator, to travel to Moscow with him to help confirm this. 'I should greatly like to have your aid and countenance in my talks with Joe ... Would you be able to let Averell come with me? I feel that things would be easier if we all seemed to be together.' He added glumly, 'I have a somewhat raw job.'[4]

The President readily agreed to Churchill's request. And the Prime Minister and Harriman set off to Moscow together. They flew from Cairo in another Liberator, one which had absolutely no sound-proofing. The two men sat side by side but the roar of the four engines was so loud that they could only communicate by passing notes to each other. Churchill's morale was made worse at lunchtime. The British Legation kitchen had supplied only ham sandwiches and when the Prime Minister shouted for mustard, the shouted reply was that there was none. Churchill in his most Edwardian tones boomed back, 'You should know that no gentleman eats ham sandwiches without mustard.'[5] (His annoyance with his staff was swept away on the return flight when he discovered that the lunch, prepared this time by the Kremlin staff, included caviar, vodka and champagne.)

The hospitality which Churchill received at the villa that was put at his disposal just outside Moscow was, he told Roosevelt, of 'totalitarian lavishness'. There were veteran servants in white jackets. There was a great dining room with a long table and sideboards bearing every drink and delicacy imaginable. The bathroom was as big as the dining room and had perpetually flowing hot and cold water. And for the travel stained Churchill it was, despite what he had said in Washington, an unforgettable pleasure to bathe there.

But his initial reception by Stalin was a vastly more uncomfortable experience. They met in the Kremlin just three hours after Churchill's arrival. Stalin was shorter and broader than his photographs suggested. He had a heavy black moustache shot with grey and wore a military tunic. His manner towards Churchill quickly became taunting, insulting. He said that the British, unlike the Russians, were clearly afraid to fight. And Harriman remembered him going on to say mockingly, 'You must not be so afraid of the Germans. You can't win wars if you aren't willing to take risks'. And at a subsequent meeting similar sneers so provoked Churchill that he could scarcely contain himself. With a great effort at self control he retorted, 'I pardon that remark only on account of the bravery of the Russian troops'.[6]

Churchill sent to Roosevelt long, detailed and vivid accounts of his meeting with Stalin. He was happy to be able to tell the President that after their early antagonisms he and Stalin had begun to warm to each other. On one occasion when Churchill became animated in discussion Stalin was both amused and impressed and 'made the remark that he liked the temperament or spirit of my utterance'. Thereafter the talk began again in a somewhat less tense atmosphere. On the last night of Churchill's visit Stalin invited him over to his private apartments in the Kremlin where they ate and drank heavily until half past three in the morning, just hours before Churchill's plane was scheduled to depart. This late night drinking session made for a lessening of antagonism between the two men. After describing it to the President Churchill concluded, 'On the whole I am definitely encouraged by my visit to Moscow'.[7]

After Churchill's return to London a principal concern for him and for Roosevelt was the forthcoming invasion by American and British forces of French North Africa. In this operation, code-named TORCH, and long urged by the Prime Minister, troops were to be landed at Casablanca on the Atlantic coast of North Africa and at Oran and Algiers on the Mediterranean shore. Roosevelt and Churchill both prepared recorded messages in French to be broadcast to reassure the population of Vichy controlled Morocco and Algeria. Roosevelt whose French was good took the opportunity to josh his friend on his notoriously fractured French, telling him and literally underlining the point '... I am making a radio disc immediately *and incidentally while your French grammar is better than mine, my accent is more alluring'*.[8]

Soon after this the personal element in the relationship was further strengthened by a goodwill visit to Britain by the President's wife Eleanor. Though emotionally and sexually estranged from her husband Eleanor was, in political matters, very close and loyal to him. Throughout the war, as earlier in the days of the New Deal, she worked tirelessly as his representative. Entrusting 'my Missus' to the care of the Churchills Roosevelt had every confidence that all would work out well. 'I know our better halves will hit it off beautifully,' he declared. And he was proved right. For though Clementine found it difficult to keep up with the punishing schedule of Eleanor's tour of Britain, she was greatly impressed by the personality of the President's wife. Writing of Eleanor's visits to young British servicewomen and women working in factories Clementine recalled, 'Each time she said something significant, fresh and true, and she gave all who heard her a sense of being in the presence of a remarkable and benevolent personality'. Clementine was also impressed by the way Eleanor Roosevelt responded to journalists. 'I was struck by the ease, friendliness and dignity with which she talked with the reporters and by the esteem and affection with which they evidently regard her.'[9]

Winston also was able to tell Roosevelt how Eleanor had won 'golden opinions here from all for her kindness and her unfailing interest in all we are doing'. But the fact remains that the friendship between the two men did not go on to become a friendship of two couples. Winston and Eleanor were not sympathetic to each other, certainly not politically. This showed up one evening at dinner at Chequers when they had a difference of opinion about the Loyalists in the Spanish Civil War. Both worked hard to be courteous to each other, in the interest of the Anglo-American alliance. But between the very liberal American woman and the old British Tory there could be no genuine warmth.

Just before Eleanor Roosevelt's return to the United States there took place the mid-term congressional elections. These proved to be a great disappointment to the President for the Republicans gained forty-four seats in the House of Representatives and nine in the Senate. Wendell Wilkie, the Republican presidential candidate in 1940, started to give indications that he might again seek the nomination. The summer and autumn had not been at all comfortable for Roosevelt. Stressed and overworked he was happiest on the weekends he spent away from Washington at Shangri-La (later renamed Camp David) a simple woodland lodge with just four bedrooms in the Maryland Hills. Here he worked on his stamp collection, played solitaire and rearranged his extensive library of books. Weariness was now beginning seriously to affect him. When Elliott Roosevelt came to see him around this time he saw in his father 'the picture of fatigue and sense of controlled strain'. Roosevelt loaned one of his books to Harry Hopkins. The choice was ominous. For the volume was an old *Book of Psalms* in which the President had marked certain passages that might be used in future speeches or that suited his present mood. One such passage was from the last verse of the thirty-ninth psalm. It read, 'O spare me, that I may recover strength, before I go hence, and be no more'.[10]

Roosevelt's demoralisation was further intensified by the setback in the mid term elections of 1942. The voters had been dissatisfied with the way manpower was being organised for the war and with factories in production. Above all they were worried by the threat of accelerating inflation in the United States. Also with the successful completion of the TORCH landings in North Africa there came, for the Allies, something of a hiatus in the war. What should be their next step? At the beginning of December 1942 Roosevelt told Churchill that 'the only satisfactory way of coming to the vital strategic conclusions the military situation requires is for you and me to meet personally with Stalin'.[11]

Roosevelt sent such an invitation to Moscow but the Soviet leader rejected it. And when Roosevelt tried again, Stalin turned him down again. At this critical moment in the Russian battle against the Germans only one matter interested Stalin and that was the second front which,

Churchill had recently told him, would not come soon.

So Roosevelt and Churchill decided they had to meet even without him. Churchill suggested Iceland but Roosevelt was put off by the climate. They then toyed with the idea of Khartoum in the Sudan which was then under British control. But they eventually decided upon Casablanca on the coast of Morocco. To meet in this city which only a couple of months before had been under Vichy control would dramatise the recent Allied victory in the TORCH landings. After his political setbacks the weary President looked forward enthusiastically to his trip. He confided to Churchill that 'it would do me personally an enormous amount of good to get out of the political atmosphere of Washington for a couple of weeks'. The meeting was arranged for the third week in the new year. Aides were sent to Casablanca to make the necessary arrangements. On Christmas Day of 1942 Roosevelt cabled Churchill, 'The Roosevelts send the Churchills warm personal greetings. The old team work is great'.

On New Year's Eve the Roosevelts threw their customary party at the White House. The movie the President specially selected as part of the night's entertainment was the very recent Warner Brothers' release starring Humphrey Bogart and Ingrid Bergman and entitled *Casablanca*, a film that would owe something of its spectacular early success to its showing around the time of the TORCH landings and the subsequent Roosevelt–Churchill meeting.

The President's feelings of anticipation intensified. The meeting was a matter of high strategic planning. But it was also a holiday. There was one slight disagreement with Churchill before the meeting and that was of a literary nature. Churchill, always concerned for secrecy and for codenames, announced that for the meeting at

Casablanca (codenamed Symbol) he would travel as Air Commodore Frankland and he asked that the President supply codenames for himself and Harry Hopkins. Roosevelt, presumably in a moment of self criticism, proposed Don Quixote for himself and Sancho Panza for Harry. Churchill was irritated by the suggestion which he found obvious and frivolous. But remembering the Spanish knight's habit of tilting at windmills, and to flatter the President politically, Churchill suggested that if Wendell Wilkie came to Casablanca, and this seemed a possibility, Wilkie should be codenamed Windmill.[12]

In the second week of January Roosevelt and his party travelled south in the presidential train, to Miami where they boarded a Boeing Clipper. The President who had been so low in spirits was now boyishly excited. He and his advisers flew first to Trinidad and then to Gambia, a small British colony on the west coast of Africa. (Roosevelt's disgust at the social conditions of the native population of Gambia would later on have an effect on his relations with Churchill.) The American party finally boarded a Douglas transport aircraft and flew on to Casablanca where Churchill and his team awaited them. With its several stop-overs the journey to Africa had taken five days.

The Prime Minister's flight to Casablanca had been most uncomfortable. On this second occasion he travelled in the Liberator *Commando*, attempts had been made to provide some heating in the plane. And the Prime Minister was able to get some sleep. But he suddenly woke up to find that his toes had been burned by one of the now red-hot heating pipes. Angrily he clambered down into the bomb bay of the aircraft to find 'two men industriously keeping alive this petrol heater'. The plane stank of petrol and, fearing 'an explosion imminent' Churchill ordered the heater turned off. 'I decided that it was better to freeze than to burn.'[13] And freeze he did. The ice cold winter air at about eight thousand feet above the North Atlantic made him shiver violently and gave him no chance of getting to sleep. He got up and struggled to pad the chilly side of the plane with blankets. His doctor tried to help, noting that 'The PM is at a disadvantage in this kind of travel, since he never wears anything at night but a silk vest. On his hands and knees, he cut a quaint figure with his big, bare, white bottom'.[14]

In such conditions did Churchill travel to the historic rendezvous in French Morocco at which he would help develop new strategies for a global war and start discussing a new political ordering of the planet after the coming of peace.

Roosevelt after his more leisurely and pleasant journey arrived in Casablanca in a buoyant, holiday mood. He was pleased with himself. He was very mindful of the four precedents he had just created in the presidency, precedents which he thought would (and indeed they did) reinvigorate the image of his own now ten-year-old presidency. He talked about the four precedents to everyone he met. He was now the first President to travel abroad in an airplane. He was the first President to leave America during a war. He was the first President since Lincoln to visit a battle theatre. He was the first President to visit Africa.

The Casablanca the President flew into was very different from that which he had seen on the film with Humphrey Bogart and Ingrid Bergman which had been shot almost entirely on Warner Brothers' lot at Burbank, California. And for the sleepless Churchill Casablanca was exhilaratingly different from the cold winter London with its blackened bombsites that he had left behind. Casablanca that January was a warm, bright, colourful place beside an ocean of dazzling blue. It was a city of gleaming, white Arab buildings built on red soil, dotted with green palms. On the seashore great white waves, sometimes fifteen feet high, foamed over the rocks. And everywhere there were richly coloured tropical flowers, crimson begonias, mauve bougainvillaea and the deep pink and white of the oleander. The place presented a dramatic contrast with the dark grey misty waters of Placentia Bay, Newfoundland where the two men had had their first conference some seventeen months before.

The Casablanca Conference was held in the Anfa Hotel which was situated on a knoll about five miles south of the city. The extensive grounds which overlooked the Atlantic Ocean and contained several luxury villas were cordoned off and heavily defended by the US Army. For though the Americans had taken the city from the Vichy French, it was still the place of intrigue depicted in the famous film. Elliott Roosevelt who had been summoned to join his father at Casablanca was very much aware of 'the small army of enemy agents and informers throughout the entire area of French Morocco. It had been only very recently that the Nazis had been driven out; the French fascists they'd left behind, with German money in their pockets, were in many cases still to be unmasked and arrested by our security forces'.[15]

As Elliott and his father got into the limousine that was to take them from the airport, American secret service men plastered the windows with the red mud of the place so that no one might see in and recognise them. There were no journalists in the procession of cars. The presence of Churchill and Roosevelt in West Africa had, as before, been kept entirely secret from the world press.

Roosevelt was to stay in one of the imposing villas in the hotel grounds and Churchill in another, some fifty yards away. Their staff members were spread out in the other villas and the hotel. Roosevelt's villa, the

Dar-es-Saada, was a very grand place with an expensively furnished living room some twenty-eight feet high and tall French windows that were covered by sliding steel curtains. (This greatly reassured the numerous security men.) Outside there was a beautiful flower garden with a large swimming pool. There were three very spacious bedrooms, two upstairs, one of which was used by Harry Hopkins and the other shared by Elliott Roosevelt and his brother Franklin Junior who had been summoned from the destroyer USS *Mayrant* on which he served as executive officer. The President's bedroom was the one on the ground floor and convenient for his wheelchair. It was, Elliott remembered, 'the bedroom of a – fairly obviously – very feminine French lady. Plenty of drapes, plenty of frills'. The bathroom had a sunken bathtub of black marble. When the President first saw all this he whistled and said, 'Now all we need is the madame of the house'.[16]

On the very evening of Roosevelt's arrival Churchill came over from his own villa, the Mirador, to see him. 'It gave me intense pleasure,' Churchill later recalled, 'to see my great colleague here on conquered or liberated territory which he and I had secured in spite of the advice given him by all his military experts.'[17] To Roosevelt this was the first day of what he regarded in part, as Harry Hopkins noted, as 'a first class holiday'. And that first evening he and Roosevelt and Churchill and those close to them relaxed and chatted and joked and reminisced together. It was all very comfortable. Elliott Roosevelt busied himself filling glasses.

The conference at Casablanca lasted about ten days and Roosevelt and Churchill were continually in each other's company. Their meetings were both formal and informal. Most formal of all were the plenary sessions in which the two leaders presided over the entire delegations which each had brought. At the first of these General Alexander of Harrow and the Guards, and very much the English gentleman, whose charm, said Churchill 'won all hearts' reported on Montgomery's campaign against Rommel in north eastern Africa. Then General Dwight Eisenhower of Abilene, Kansas, and West Point who had a very short haircut and a nervous, clipped way of speaking reported on the progress of the American forces after the TORCH landings which he had commanded. Eisenhower was much criticised in the United States and Britain at this time for the understandings he had come to with Vichy France in North Africa. A reconciliation between the former Vichy authorities now headed by General Giraud and the Free French headquartered in London and led by General Charles de Gaulle was one of the tasks of the Casablanca conference.

Three days later all the uniformed military men and political advisers on both sides came together in the hotel's white, Arab style ballroom for the second plenary session. On this crowded occasion Churchill felt it necessary to declare publicly to the President that when Hitler was defeated, Britain would not drop out of the war. She would continue to fight alongside the Americans in the Pacific. He promised that 'all of the British resources and effort will be turned towards the defeat of Japan. Not only were British interests involved, but also, he added, with a Churchillian throb and flourish 'her honour is engaged'.

Between plenary sessions the two military staffs worked on both larger and lesser issues of world strategy for this New Year of 1943. The American team was at first somewhat wary of the British. The Americans had no clear plans and were indeed divided among themselves about what would be the next best initiative in the war. They suspected that the British had a very definite agenda. And they also thought that their senior officers such as Generals Marshall and Eisenhower, with their soft, slow way of speaking, could be 'outsmarted' by the likes of General Alan Brooke, the Ulsterman with an incisive mind and a habit of arrogance, 'an Irishman with an Irishman's quickness' who could on occasion offend the American officers with 'his swift, abrupt speech, his downright categorical expression of his views and occasional impatience'.[18] But gradually the difference in British and American style came to matter less, and with promptings from Churchill and from Roosevelt above, definite agreements began to be worked out. It was established conclusively that there would be no further consideration of a landing of any kind in France that year. It was also settled, after lengthy discussion that with North Africa won, the Allies would invade Sicily. The war against U-boats in the North Atlantic, the Pacific war and assistance to the Soviet Union were also confirmed as prime commitments.

Harry Hopkins was at first disappointed with the results from the Conference. He told Churchill that 'it seemed to me like a pretty feeble effort for two great countries in 1943'.[19] He had expected far more. But when he read the first document prepared by the Combined Chiefs of Staff he was converted to the view of the President and the Prime Minister that it was 'the most complete strategic plan for a world-wide war that had ever been conceived – far exceeding the accomplishments of the last war'.

The day after the third and final plenary session at which the last details of the communiquè were worked out, some fifty astonished journalists were brought to Casablanca for a press conference. Before questions began, Churchill later recalled, 'de Gaulle and Giraud were made to sit in a row of chairs alternating with the

President and me' so that the two Frenchmen so hostile to each other might be photographed together. Roosevelt even prevailed upon the two enemies to shake hands in front of the cameras. For Churchill the sight of the haughty, troublesome, sullen de Gaulle, for so long an irritation in the Prime Minister's life, making this gesture, remained a source of amusement. Years later he wrote that 'the pictures of this event cannot be viewed even in the setting of these tragic times without a laugh'.[20]

But shortly after the two French generals had stomped off in different directions, Churchill's secret laughter was ended by a sudden and intense anger. It was provoked by the President. It occurred as he and Roosevelt continued to talk to the journalists. It was one of the worst moments in all the years of his relationship with Roosevelt.

What so galled Churchill was the President's announcement to the pressmen that the Allies were now committed to a policy of Unconditional Surrender. In effect there would be no further negotiations with Fascists such as those which Eisenhower had undertaken with Vichy in North Africa. Germany, Japan and Italy would not be allowed to attend a peace conference of any kind. This war would not end with any kind of Versailles Treaty such as ended the First World War. The Axis powers would be required to surrender without any reservations whatsoever.

As the President made this historic declaration to the press, Churchill, sitting beside him gave every appearance of being calm and very much a party to it. But internally he was boiling with rage. And when Churchill met Harriman after the press conference had ended, the Prime Minister was still in a terrible temper. 'He was in high dudgeon,' Harriman remembered, 'offended that Roosevelt should have made such a momentous announcement without prior consultation ... I had seen him unhappy with Roosevelt more than once, but this time he was more deeply offended than before'.[21]

Roosevelt later suggested that the principle of Unconditional Surrender just 'popped into' his head. But there is evidence to suggest that he had been considering it for a long time and even that he had discussed the matter with Churchill. The Prime Minister's anger with his friend seems more likely to derive from the manner rather than the content of the President's announcement to the press. It was Churchill's personal pride rather than his political position that had been hurt. His dignity had been offended. As Harriman judged, 'Churchill's dismay, it would appear, had less to do with the principle of unconditional surrender than with the fact that Roosevelt had proclaimed it on his own'. As the war progressed and the primacy of the American contribution to the Allied cause grew every day more obvious, the maintaining of a partnership and friendship with Roosevelt became an ever more delicate matter for Churchill. Friendship, comradeship could easily fall away and Churchill find himself the side kick, the sycophant, the hanger-on.

The press conference at Casablanca was certainly a blow to the relationship. But the upset was temporary. And undoubtedly the ten day African conference as a whole developed and strengthened the friendship. The many occasions on which the two men met privately and socially were, despite one comic exception, extremely successful. Roosevelt, Hopkins and Churchill had all brought sons to Casablanca and there was a family feeling to the socialising. There was a good deal of toing and froing between the two villas. In Roosevelt's, one observer recalled, there was 'a general atmosphere of extraordinarily good will ... talk by the hour' and 'an enormous quantity of highballs'.[22] Elliott Roosevelt was pleased and relieved to see the effect that life at Casablanca was having on his father. 'The change was doing him good despite the heavy schedule; he looked fit; some of the grayness was disappearing from his cheeks.' And over in his villa the Prime Minister insisted on the holiday aspect to the Conference. When not sitting in on the negotiations he joked and played cards, 'ate and drank enormously and generally enjoyed himself'.

During the conference the two men took turns in hosting each other for the evening dinner. Roosevelt greatly enjoyed visiting Churchill's War Room in the Villa Mirador in which were set up large and highly detailed maps of every theatre of the war. On his several visits the President was especially interested in the map of the U-boat war in the North Atlantic. It elicited in him a heady feeling of being involved in a global epic. With Churchill he recalled the epics of Greece and of Rome. But the present one was so much vaster. As his son, Elliott, said, 'the suspense that was engendered in the tiny pins and miniatures of that Admiralty map was a global suspense, with the answer to world history caught up in its resolution'.[23]

But the visits were usually more light-hearted. On one evening visit to Churchill Roosevelt's party included some black GIs who, after dinner sang spirituals and a version of 'Danny Boy' which moved the Prime Minister greatly. It was after this dinner that Churchill telegraphed Anthony Eden, deputising for him in London, his sense of an increased intimacy with Roosevelt. 'He is in great form,' Churchill reported, 'and we have never been so close.' In the same wire Churchill echoed something of the imperial manner of Roosevelt's presidency when he added, 'He has gone up the line today to inspect his troops'. This was the occasion on which Roosevelt drove eighty-five miles north east of Casablanca to visit, and to be photographed with soldiers from General Mark Clark's

Fifth Army. With studied informality he lunched in the open with them, eating boiled ham and sweet potatoes. Music to dine by was supplied by an artillery band and was similarly American. Into the vast expanses of the desert the brass instruments blared out 'Deep In The Heart of Texas', 'The Missouri Waltz' and 'Chattanooga Choo Choo'.

The President's journey to and from his army was supervised by dozens of security officers responsible for his safety. Throughout the Casablanca Conference the participants bore in mind the possibility that some Fascist organisation might attempt an attack on the hotel compound. Churchill continually urged that they change the venue, proposing Marrakech, some miles to the south, as a safer place. One evening after the President had hosted the dinner and he and the Prime Minister and a few companions sat drinking and talking the alarm was actually sounded. It was half-past one in the morning. All the lights in that high-ceilinged room were immediately switched off. Six small candles were brought in and the relaxed conversation continued on into the small hours. To one of those present, the Irishman Alan Brooke, the strong, characterful profiles of Roosevelt and Churchill seen in that weak, flickering orange light would remain an image not to be forgotten.

All the evening dinners were highly congenial, except one. That one exception was the occasion on which Roosevelt entertained Churchill along with the Sultan of Morocco. The Sultan in his flowing robes of white silk sought to ingratiate himself with the President in the hopes that the United States might give economic and financial assistance to his country. The Sultan spoke at great length about his reservations concerning French imperial rule in Morocco. And he craftily sought to encourage the President to give his views of imperialism. None of this was, of course, to Churchill's taste and he sat silent and gloomy. Roosevelt was amused at his friend's uneasiness but kept a straight face. The President could be amused by the discomforts of others however much he might be attached to them. And such amusement flickered in his eyes that evening as he sat there in his tuxedo, puffing on the cigarette in his cigarette holder and slowly and thoughtfully reviewing the wrongs of imperial systems.

And for Churchill there was an even greater unpleasantness at that particular dinner. Islamic law required that no alcohol be consumed in the Sultan's presence. The Prime Minister's mood grew steadily worse. Unlike Harry Hopkins, who had taken the precaution of fortifying himself with some drinks before dinner, Churchill was not even amused by the gifts which the Sultan had brought. Harry Hopkins remembered that these included 'a gold dagger for the President, and gold bracelets for Mrs Roosevelt and a gold tiara which looked to me like the kind the gals wear in the circus, riding on white horses'. Harry added, 'I can just see Mrs Roosevelt when she takes a look at this'.[24]

For once Churchill left a dinner party early. He was greatly irritated. But later he felt compensated when Roosevelt agreed to share with him what Churchill regarded as an opportune occasion for a quiet time together. This was a visit to Marrakech, the Moroccan city looking out on to the Atlas Mountains which Churchill had visited and been entranced by, on a visit a few years before the war began. He told Roosevelt, 'You cannot come all this way to North Africa without seeing Marrakech. Let us spend two days there. I must be with you when you see the sunset on the snows of the Atlas Mountains'. And with that Edwardian, slightly suggestive worldliness that always intrigued and entertained Roosevelt Churchill went on to paint a verbal picture of what he called 'the Paris of the Sahara'. It was the place 'where all the caravans had come from Central Africa for centuries to be heavily taxed en route by the tribes in the mountains and afterwards swindled in the Marrakech market, receiving the return, which they greatly valued, of the gay life of the city, including fortune-tellers, snake-charmers, masses of food and drink, and on the whole the largest and most elaborately organised brothels in the African continent. All these institutions were of long and ancient repute'.[25]

But it was also Churchill the artist as well as Churchill the man of the world who so persistently urged the visit on Roosevelt. The Atlas Mountains viewed from Marrakech were, the Prime Minister insisted, the most beautiful sight in the whole world. They would also be a great shared memory between them. Roosevelt finally accepted Churchill's appeals and agreed to go, though only for one day. Elaborate preparations were made.

The moment the conference was over, they set off. The security was intense and elaborate. The journey was a matter of a hundred and fifty miles and every two hundred yards or so along the road there stood an armed American soldier. And above the cavalcade of cars there was a large and noisy escort of fighters from the United States Air Force. The drive to Marrakech took some four hours, one of the longest periods Roosevelt and Churchill spent alone together. The Prime Minister recalled that they 'talked a great deal of shop, but also touched on lighter matters'. Their destination was the Villa Taylor, a luxury home owned by a wealthy American but presently housing a young American archaeologist who had served as a secret agent for US Intelligence prior to the TORCH landings. The white villa was in an ornate Moroccan style and situated in the middle of what had once been an olive grove.

The party arrived as dusk was beginning and Churchill immediately and enthusiastically climbed up on to the roof of the villa to see the glowing pink sunset over the long range of the Atlas Mountains rising up from out of the desert. And, as on that first visit in the thirties, Churchill was greatly moved. He hurried back down to the ground floor and urged passionately that the President allow himself to be brought up to the roof to see the amazing landscape.

Compelled by the power of Churchill's enthusiasm Roosevelt, although shy and uneasy about his disability, agreed to climb up. So two servants made a chair with their arms and, with some difficulty, struggled him up on to the roof. It was a moment (like that in which Roosevelt had insisted that Churchill feel his biceps) of sudden physical awareness between the two men. One onlooker was both shocked and sympathetic when he saw the physical condition of the President of the United States, as Roosevelt 'was carried up the winding stairs to the roof-top, his paralysed legs dangling like the limbs of a ventriloquist's dummy, limp and flaccid'.[26]

For some time the two friends sat and gazed at the line of snowy mountains where the light changed to a different shade of purple every minute.

Later, after the President had been carried down to his room, Churchill went for a stroll with Lord Moran among the now twilit orange trees in the garden of the villa. The Prime Minister reminisced about the happenings at the Casablanca Conference and seemed well pleased with it and especially with his times with Roosevelt. Suddenly he stopped walking and turned to Moran and burst out, 'I love these Americans. They have behaved so generously'.[27]

Such good feeling continued and grew at the very last dinner party later that evening. Churchill and Roosevelt made informal and very affectionate speeches to each other. And there was great camaraderie among all those present for this occasion together. 'We had a very jolly dinner,' Churchill remembered, 'and we all sang songs. I sang and the President joined in the choruses, and at one moment was about to try a solo. However, someone interrupted and I never heard this.'

The party lasted until two in the morning. The President and the other Americans had to be up before seven for their flight from Marrakech airport. Roosevelt said his goodbyes to Churchill as the dinner party broke up. But on rising, early the following morning, the President decided to go and take his leave one more time. He found Churchill in bed. The Prime Minister started up and insisted that he would accompany Roosevelt to the airport. Churchill pulled on his zipper suit over his flamboyant silk dressing gown with the red dragons on it. Then he found his slippers and flapped his way down to the President's car. He rode with him to the airport runway. Here he helped push his friend's wheelchair up to the special ramp into the transport aircraft.

After their final farewells inside the plane, Churchill emerged and remained to watch the take-off. The stocky little figure in the blue zip suit, slippers and dressing gown stayed to watch as the President's plane flew off, grew smaller and smaller and finally disappeared in the pink desert light of early morning.

Churchill returned to the Villa Taylor and pondered what had happened over the last ten days politically and personally. His doctor sensed that he was reluctant to break the illusion of being on holiday. Nevertheless the Prime Minister exchanged communications with the War Cabinet in London, trying to get its members to agree to a daring new personal initiative which he had in mind. But the Cabinet feared for him and argued with him, asking him to take no further risks in flying.

As he awaited the outcome of these exchanges, Churchill climbed back up to the roof of the villa where he had sat with the President. For a long time he studied the

Atlas Mountains which were all the time brightening as the sun rose higher. Then he took out his paints and brushes and began a picture. This was the only painting he attempted during the war. He intended to send it to Roosevelt as a remembrance.

Notes

1. Gilbert, p. 138.
2. Ibid., p. 140.
3. Lord Moran, *Winston Churchill: The Struggle for Survival 1940–1965* (Constable, 1966), p. 49.
4. Kimball, p. 553.
5. W. Averell Harriman and Elie Abel, *Special Envoy to Churchill and Stalin 1941–46* (New York, Random House, 1975), p. 152.
6. Ibid., p. 157.
7. Kimball, p. 571.
8. Ibid., p. 630.
9. Mary Soames, *Clementine Churchill* (Cassell, 1979), p. 318.
10. Robert E. Sherwood, *Roosevelt and Hopkins: An Intimate History* (New York, Harper Brothers, 1948), p. 626.
11. Kimball, Vol II, p. 54.
12. Ibid., p. 109.
13. Churchill, p. 605.
14. Moran, p. 79.
15. Elliott Roosevelt, p. 62.
16. Ibid., p. 65.
17. Churchill, p. 605.
18. Bryant, p. 451.
19. Sherwood, p. 691.
20. Churchill, p. 62.
21. Harriman, p. 188.
22. Gilbert, p. 306.
23. Elliott Roosevelt, p. 64.
24. Sherwood, p. 689.
25. Churchill, p. 622.
26. Moran, p. 82.
27. Ibid., p. 82.

6 Reassurances and Recitations

After they returned from the tropics to a wintery Washington and to an even more wintery London, the two elderly friends fell seriously ill. When the President flew off from Marrakech on the bright early morning, he travelled first to Bathurst a hot, steamy riverside town in the British colony of Gambia. Roosevelt had for many years been an avid reader of the *National Geographic* magazine, and was always curious about the world. And he now insisted on a trip up the humid Gambia River. He was to remember this journey by river tugboat as a voyage into the heart of darkness and he soon started to feel unwell. He later told Churchill, 'I think I picked up sleeping sickness or Gambia fever or some kindred bug in that hell-hole of your so called Bathurst. It laid me low – four days in bed …' He struggled to resume his duties as President but the drugs which cured his fever left him 'feeling like a wet rag' and after two o'clock in the afternoon he simply could not function. After a week of this he felt compelled to give up on Washington and all his many responsibilities. He went home to Hyde Park and had five days of total rest but was then able to report to Churchill that 'I have been feeling like a fighting cock ever since'.[1]

A far more life threatening illness lay in wait for the

Prime Minister on his return to London. He had stayed away from home far longer than the President had done. For when he left Marrakech he had finally prevailed on his War Cabinet to agree to what its members regarded as his wild and dangerous escapade of flying east across Africa to meet secretly with the President of Turkey and to try to recruit him and his country to the Allied cause. After this finally unproductive meeting in a railway train on a remote siding in south eastern Turkey, Churchill turned homewards flying via North Africa where, in the intense heat, he made stirring speeches to the British troops who had recently completed the great victory over the Germans in that theatre. He was back in bitterly cold England at the end of the first week in February. Within days he became extremely unwell and just over a week later pneumonia was diagnosed.

Ordered to bed by his doctor Churchill reluctantly attempted to rest. He decided to indulge his literary interests and give himself the treat of reading Daniel Defoe's *Moll Flanders*. But except when he was totally incapacitated by his illness, he found it impossible to give up on the many tasks that went with political and military leadership. Over in Washington Franklin Roosevelt, himself so very recently recovered from illness, worried greatly about his friend's condition. At this time there came a kind of fellow feeling into their correspondence: the highly particularised sympathy of those with recent and immediate experience of incapacitating illness. In one of his messages to Churchill the President implored, 'Please, please, for the sake of the world, don't overdo it these days. You must remember that it takes about a month of occasional let-ups to get back your full strength'. And he concluded, 'Tell Mrs Churchill that when I was laid up I was a thoroughly model patient and that I hope you will live down the reputation in our Press of having been the "world's worst patient". God bless you. As ever yours, Franklin D. Roosevelt.'

In these difficult times the two movie enthusiasts were able to share an especial pleasure in the film *Desert Victory* which depicted Montgomery's successful campaign in North Africa. Just as he started to recover Churchill sent a print of the film by plane to Roosevelt. In an accompanying note he said how impressed he had been by the film's 'vivid and realistic picture of the battles'. Churchill also quietly alluded to that memorable moment of closeness in Washington on the day of the fall of Tobruk and Roosevelt's spontaneous gift of American Sherman tanks. Churchill noted, without further remark, 'I know that you will be interested in the photographs of your Sherman tanks in action'. In a 'Dear Winston' letter the President responded enthusiastically, 'That new film *Desert Victory* is about the best thing that has been done about the war on either side. Everyone here is enthusiastic. I gave a special showing for the White House Staff and tonight the Interior Department employees are having a special showing because everybody is talking about it; and I understand that within ten days it will be in the picture houses. Great good will be done.'

In this March of 1943 the relations between the two men could not have been better. But in the larger military and political ordering of the alliance strains were beginning to develop. As the spring came on, the unity seemingly achieved in 'the spirit of Casablanca' started to fragment. Relations between General Giraud and General de Gaulle, whom the Americans regarded as a protegé of the British, proved to be a serious problem. After the handshake at Casablanca Roosevelt hoped for the best from the bride and bridegroom as he called them. He told Churchill, 'I take it that your bride and my bridegroom have not yet started throwing the crockery. I trust the marriage will be consummated'. But numerous, bitter hostilities developed between the two French generals in the administration of the French colonies. And at last in a lengthy memorandum Roosevelt angrily criticised Churchill's client, the bride, de Gaulle. 'I am sorry but it seems to me the conduct of the BRIDE continues to be more and more aggravated. His course and attitude is well nigh intolerable ... De Gaulle may be an honest fellow but he has the Messianic complex ... All in all, I think you and I should thrash out this disagreeable problem and establish a common policy'.[2]

Another growing tension within the Anglo-American alliance had to do with Eisenhower's desire to delay the invasion of Sicily. This greatly irritated Churchill who believed strongly that the western allies owed it to the Russians to be militarily engaged with the Axis at all times and to allow no delays and inactivity. But perhaps the most serious new rift in the alliance had to do with Tube Alloys, the project which would lead to the creating of an atomic bomb. Earlier it had been agreed that Britain and America would cooperate as equals in this programme but Churchill's advisers now informed him that the Americans were no longer sharing their research with their ally. Initially, as he so often did, Churchill took up this vital matter with Harry Hopkins rather than with the President and told him that 'if the full pooling of information on progress in nuclear fission were not resumed, then Britain would be compelled to go ahead separately in this work'. And that, as Churchill emphasised, would be 'a sombre decision'.[3]

Increasingly worried by these and other 'serious divergences beneath the surface' Churchill proposed that he again visit the President in Washington.[4] The Prime Minister had his way. Four calendar months to the day after leaving Casablanca he embarked on the Cunard liner

Queen Mary for the port of New York. His doctor did not want him to endure the discomforts of a military aircraft so soon after his pneumonia. And the more comfortable Boeing Clippers could not take off because of late ice. So Churchill decided to risk the dangers of the North Atlantic and travel by sea. It was the fifth of his long journeys to meet Roosevelt.

After travelling up to Scotland in his special train Churchill boarded the *Queen Mary* at Greenock on the Clyde. The interior of the famous ship had been stripped down so that it might serve as a troopship in both the Atlantic and the Pacific. Even now it was in the process of being deloused after one such voyage. But the luxury fittings were restored to the main deck which was taken over by Churchill and his large party. Looking down on the lower decks he and his companions could see the thousands of captured Germans and Italians in their prisoner-of-war uniforms with round patches on the back and knee. These men who had surrendered in North Africa were bound, via New York, to prison camps in Canada.

In late afternoon the great Cunarder, with its two tiers of passengers, set off, holding close to the Ayrshire coast with the dark green hills of the Islands of Bute and Arran showing up in the bright spring light to starboard. As the liner steamed out into the Atlantic the passengers had a fine view of the spectacular line of rocks known as the Giant's Causeway on the coast of Northern Ireland. Not long after the *Queen Mary* was joined by her escort ships, a cruiser and an aircraft-carrier. A Sunderland flying boat patrolled overhead.

On board the liner the Prime Minister kept his staff hard at work on formulating the positions to be taken on the various complex issues of strategy and supply that were going to be negotiated with the Americans. But in the evenings Churchill enjoyed relaxing in his large suite, the one area in an otherwise 'dry' ship which was, on his insistence, definitely not 'dry'. As on other historic journeys undertaken by Churchill there was a sense of vacation as well as of high purpose. He was, as Averell Harriman who travelled with him remembered, 'in holiday spirits throughout the voyage'. He enjoyed his food and drink, and cards and conversation. He chaffed his Canadian friend, the newspaper proprietor and writer, Lord Beaverbrook, about matters of English prose style, calling for a copy of Fowler's *Modern English Usage* and declaiming passages from it. He joked and boasted about what he would do if they were torpedoed by a U-boat. But along with all his advisers he was greatly pleased when, on the day the British escort ships turned back, there appeared on the horizon a large number of escort vessels from the United States Navy. It was an imposing flotilla of two cruisers and four destroyers. Air surveillance and rescue possibilities were provided by a Catalina flying boat. Flattered and moved by the impressiveness of this reception Churchill cabled the President, 'Since yesterday we have been surrounded by US Navy and we all greatly appreciate high value evidently set upon our continued survival'.[5]

The *Queen Mary* and her tugs entered the port of New York in a heavy mist and the members of the British delegation, all standing out on the main deck, had a disappointingly poor view of the Statue of Liberty and the Manhattan skyline. The liner berthed at Staten Island and Harry Hopkins, looking as if he had slept in his suit, bustled on board to welcome the visitors. He then escorted them to the train that was to take them south to Washington DC. As they sped along through New Jersey they had lunch in the dining car. One item on the menu was 'small steaks' which every single member of the

British party eagerly ordered. When the steaks arrived they proved to be far larger than a whole week's meat ration for an adult back in Britain. The visitors were outfaced by the steaks. One British officer, well known as a trencherman, said regretfully, 'We were out of practice'.[6]

The train steamed into the grand, soaring interior of Washington's Union Station, an interior modelled on the baths of Diocletian in Rome. (Its granite entrance was copied from the Arch of Constantine.) Most of the station was cordoned off. And as Churchill looked out on to the broad marble platform, he was moved to see a familiar figure seated in his wheelchair awaiting him. They greeted each other warmly. Then Churchill rode with the President in his Cadillac surrounded by a large motor-cycle escort to the White House where he was given his usual room. All the other members of the British delegation were lodged at the Statler Hotel.

The following afternoon this third Washington conference, codenamed Trident, got underway in the Oval Office in the White House. Those assembled, most of them in military uniforms, heard introductory speeches first from the Prime Minister and then from the President. In the two weeks the Trident meeting lasted there was to be a good deal of tension between the two delegations. Many Americans were sceptical about Churchill's ambition to invade Italy after the capture of Sicily. They were less interested in further Mediterranean campaigns than in an invasion of northern France leading to a more direct assault on Germany. And some Americans wanted to de-emphasise the European war altogether in order to concentrate on the struggle with the Japanese in the Pacific. One such advocate was the stiff, unbending, somewhat gauche Admiral Stark, a macho type who, Roosevelt maintained, was so tough that he shaved with a blow torch. Another was the aggressive and abrasive General 'Vinegar Joe' Stilwell who was violently anti-British. Stilwell complained bitterly about what he regarded as British dilatoriness in fighting the war in Asia, maintaining that Churchill had Roosevelt 'in his pocket'.

If there were tensions horizontally across the negotiating table, there were also tensions vertically between the two leaders and their subordinates. Churchill in particular had some serious disagreements with his military advisers. But between Churchill and Roosevelt themselves whatever disagreements there may have been were carefully muted or understated. The way in which they managed their friendship prevented confrontation. The practical consequence was that the Trident conference shelved, or put on hold, certain difficult issues. As with other conferences its importance lay, in great part, in the continuing process of alliance rather than in firm, definitive formulations of policy on all issues.

After some three days of difficult, often frustrating negotiations, there came the week-end and a respite for the two teams. Senior British officers were taken by their American counterparts to visit Williamsburg, the capital of Virginia in the eighteenth century which John D. Rockefeller had, in the 1920s, at great cost, restored to the way it had been in colonial and revolutionary times. The British visitors were intrigued to see local people in eighteenth century dress moving about beautifully restored shops and offering the food and goods of the time. They visited the old Virginia Capitol building restored according to Thomas Jefferson's plans for remodelling. They also patronised the restored tavern, *The King's Arms*, which after Washington's final defeat of the British was renamed *The Eagle*.

While the Prime Minister's advisers enjoyed themselves in Williamsburg, he himself was the President's personal guest at Shangri-La, his rural retreat in the Maryland Hills. They were accompanied by the President's wife Eleanor and Harry Hopkins. As they emerged from the White House and prepared to get into the presidential limousine the forceful Eleanor insisted that Winston should sit at the back with her husband. She would sit with Harry on one of the lower seats behind the chauffeur. With a gallant, Edwardian bow Winston, homburg hat in hand, insisted that her place was beside her husband; he, Winston, would sit in front. Eleanor would not have this; Winston insisted. The President and Harry Hopkins already seated in the car looked on anxiously as the altercation continued ever more insistently between two people whose feeling for each other was, as was well known, not deep. After several minutes of argument Eleanor gave way and sat beside her husband.

Surrounded by its armed motorcycle escort the President's Cadillac sped out into the rolling Maryland countryside. As they approached the small town of Frederick Churchill's attention was attracted by a billboard advertising Barbara Frietchie candies. The name rang a bell, he said, Who was the lady? Harry Hopkins explained that she had been an old lady at the time of the American Civil War who was a great supporter of Abraham Lincoln and the North. Her house always flew the Union flag. One day, when Confederate troops, led up from the South by General Stonewall Jackson, had marched into the town of Frederick, they had fired at and damaged the Union flag that hung from Barbara Frietchie's window. But the ninety-year-old lady had thrown open her window and shouted defiantly at the Southern general and his troops. 'There's a famous poem about her,' Harry continued. 'By John Greenleaf Whittier'. And he recited the lines containing Barbara Frietchie's

brave words to Stonewall Jackson and his southern army:
' Shoot if you must, this old gray head,/But spare your
country's flag,'' she said.' Harry tried to remember more
of the poem but could not.

And then something happened which astonished the
three Americans and which they never forgot. For as they
drove through the streets of Frederick Winston Churchill
began to declaim.

> 'Up from the meadows rich with corn
> Clear in the cool September morn,
> The clustered spires of Frederick stand.'

And then missing out some thirteen lines and
misremembering the heroine's age, he continued:

> 'Up rose old Barbara Frietchie then,
> Bowed with her threescore years and ten
> Bravest of all in Frederick town
> She took up the flag that the men had hauled down.'

Then skippping six lines he came to the dramatic
moment in which the Confederate soldiers shot at the
Union flag.

> 'Halt! The dust-brown ranks stood fast.
> Fire! Out blazed the rifle-blast.
> It shivered the window, pane and sash.
> It rent the banner with many a gash.
> Quick as it fell from the broken staff
> Dame Barbara seized the silken scarf.
> She leaned far out of the window-sill
> And shook it forth with a right good will.
> "Shoot, if you must, this old gray head
> But spare your country's flag," she said.'

Clearly very pleased with himself Churchill went on to
recite the lines describing Stonewall Jackson's reaction.

'A shade of sadness, a touch of shame
Over the face of the leader came,
And a nobler nature within him stirred
At the sight of this woman's deed and word.
"Who touches a hair of yon grey head
Dies like a dog! March on!" he said.
So all day long through Frederick's street
Sounded the tramp of marching feet,
And all day long that free flag tossed
Over the heads of the rebel host.'

As he concluded, and afterwards basked in the admiration and astonishment of his companions Churchill said that he had not thought of Whittier's poem for more than thirty years. And now a billboard in Maryland had brought it all back. As a young man he had memorised a great deal of English poetry. (To entertain Violet Asquith, the daughter of the Edwardian Prime Minister who had first given him Cabinet office, he had memorised all the odes of Keats.) But he had long forgotten that he had committed to memory Whittier's poem of the American Civil War.

The green Maryland countryside through which the Presidential party was now passing was full of associations with that war. They saw a road sign pointing to Gettysburg. And Churchill quite high on his literary triumph entertained his friends with a long account of the Battle of Gettysburg and of the characters of Robert E. Lee and Stonewall Jackson who had at the last behaved so gallantly to Barbara Frietchie by allowing her to fly her flag. Again Churchill's listeners were greatly impressed by the range and details of Churchill's knowledge.

Some days later in a speech before Congress Churchill would mention the battlefield of Gettysburg, noting that it was a field 'which I know well like most of your battlefields'. And this was indeed the case. Fourteen years before when out of office and trying to make money as a writer Churchill had gone to Hollywood to try to interest Charlie Chaplin in a filmscript about Napoleon. When he returned to the east coast he studied and tramped over all the major battlefields of the Civil War in preparation for another writing project he had in mind.

The weekend at Shangri-La was quiet, intimate and restful. It made for still further bonding between the two men. Upon arrival they had a quiet time together, after Roosevelt had ordered his aide General 'Pa' Watson, a fat raconteur and clown, to bring all the paraphernalia of his stamp collection to him. Always a little breathless Watson, whose role at the White House was chiefly to serve as Roosevelt's court jester, struggled in with several large albums, a magnifying glass and a pile of envelopes full of stamps. Churchill sat with the President for a long time, silently watching as he lost himself in studying the stamps and carefully fixing them in their proper places in his albums. The only sound in that simply furnished room, scented by the timber of its walls, was the sound of the clock ticking. Churchill watched the President grow ever more relaxed.

But then came the sound of a car driving up the hill to the cabin. A door slammed and in rushed General Bedell Smith from General Eisenhower's headquarters in North Africa. He had questions that required answers urgently. So, with a sad shake of the head, Roosevelt had to turn aside from his calming hobby and become the commander in chief again.

After a leisurely breakfast on Sunday Roosevelt invited Churchill to go fishing with him in one of the several streams that flowed through the beautiful woods surrounding Shangri-La. The streams on the estate were full of fine trout. Churchill readily accepted the invitation and a little party which included Eleanor, 'Pa' Watson and some other aides who carried the President, made their way through the trees, just now taking on their summer green, to the stream. They came to a place where it opened out into a pool and here the aides carefully placed the President. Eleanor took a photograph of her husband with Churchill. The President wore a sweater and an open-necked shirt. But Churchill was of a nation and a generation that were unaccustomed to such casual style. The British Prime Minister week-ending by a trout stream wore his overcoat and his homburg hat.

Churchill wandered about with his fishing rod trying various places by the pool and by the stream. There was birdsong in the woods. Churchill caught nothing and neither did the President. But Churchill saw that his friend had 'the first quality of an angler which is not to measure the pleasure by the catch'. He could also see Roosevelt's happiness in simply being by the pool. Quietness and relaxation were increasingly precious to him.

On the Monday morning both men were regretful about having to leave what Churchill called 'this agreeable cool abode' for the 'really great heat of Washington'. On the drive back through the town of Frederick Churchill asked if there could be a detour to enable him to see the house of Barbara Frietchie. And as they stopped outside it and Harry Hopkins repeated the two lines he knew, all four members of the party recaptured some of the pleasure and excitement of the outward journey.

After his return to Washington Churchill made his speech to the Congress. He praised recent Allied victories which clearly constituted a milestone in the war. But Gettysburg had been a milestone also. And, he reminded his audience, 'far more blood was shed after the Union victory at Gettysburg than in all the fighting which went before'. In the present war, Churchill insisted, the maximum unremitting effort was still necessary. Roosevelt listened to the speech on the radio in the White House. When Churchill returned he was happy to see how 'very pleased' his host was with him.[7]

What gave the President far less pleasure was the tolerance which the British continued to show to de Gaulle, a figure whom Roosevelt came more and more to resent. The President broached the matter most tactfully but Churchill was in no doubt about his anger. Of Roosevelt's criticism of the Free French leader Churchill wrote, 'Although this was done in a most friendly and often jocular manner, I saw he felt very strongly indeed upon it'. Jokes rather than confrontation were the way in which the relationship between Roosevelt and Churchill was safeguarded. And both men were keenly aware of the practical political importance of its safeguarding. At this Trident conference, for instance, the friendship was instrumental in easing an important tension between Britain and the United States again on the issue of Tube Alloys, the development of a nuclear weapon. Certainly Harry Hopkins was very skilful in dealing with British grievances but the main push came from Roosevelt himself after conversations with Churchill. The Prime Minister prided himself on this example of the force of the friendship and its power to sweep aside divisions among British and American Staff officers. 'The fact that the President and I had been living side by side seeing each other at all hours, that we were known to be in close agreement, and that the President intended to decide himself on the ultimate issues – all this ... exercised throughout a mollifying and also a dominating influence on the course of Staff discussions.'[8]

A conference decision that pleased the Americans was the commitment to a cross Channel invasion of Europe in a year's time in May of 1944. A decision that was not pleasing to Churchill was the decision, which was essentially Roosevelt's, not to make, as yet, a commitment to the invasion of Italy after victory in Sicily. Beset by conflicting arguments the President, as he often did, procrastinated. Churchill suggested that it might be useful if he, Churchill, went to discuss possibilities with Eisenhower on the spot, at his headquarters in North Africa. The President consented to this and also to Churchill's request that General George Marshall, the American Chief of Staff, accompany him. The Prime Minister did not wish to give the impression of treating with Eisenhower without the presence of a senior American official.

And so, after two weeks, Trident came to an end. The weather was now warm enough for Churchill to travel by Boeing Clipper. And early in the morning of 26 May Churchill and Roosevelt drove down to the Potomac River where the plane was anchored. As the rest of the party went on board the two men said their extended and affectionate goodbyes in the President's limousine.

It was typical of the high drama and danger of Churchill's wartime journeyings that the great silver aircraft should, some hours out over the Atlantic, be violently knocked off its course by an immense stroke of lightning.

Notes

1. Kimball, p. 156.
2. Ibid., p. 210.
3. Sherwood, p. 704.
4. Gilbert, p. 394.
5. Kimball, p. 212.
6. Ismay, p. 295.
7. Churchill, p. 714.
8. Ibid., p. 715.

7   Being Made at Home

The closeness of the two men during this third Washington meeting is indicated by the warmth of the messages they exchanged after parting. Just two days after Churchill flew off the President cabled him, 'I miss you much. It was a highly successful meeting in every way and proved that it was well timed and necessary'. And Churchill in thanking the President and Mrs Roosevelt for 'your great kindness and hospitality' goes on to say that he carried away 'the most pleasant memories' and concludes with the short strong sentence, 'You know how I value your friendship'. And in a speech in which he reported to the House of Commons about his American visit Churchill said, 'My own relations with the illustrious President of the United States have become in these years of war those of personal friendship and regard, and nothing will ever happen to separate us in comradeship and partnership of thought and action....'[1]

Churchill who returned to London via North Africa reported to Roosevelt that he had been greatly pleased with his talks with General Eisenhower in Algiers. And as a man with a strong sense of history and antiquity Churchill took special pleasure in addressing the victorious British troops of the African campaign in the sun-whitened Roman amphitheatre in Carthage.

But for Roosevelt in Washington there was at this time no cause for exhilaration. Indeed as the summer of 1943 went by the friendship was further reinforced by Churchill's understanding and sympathy for what it is like to be head of a government in trouble. That summer very little went right for Roosevelt; there was a succession of blunders and failures. In late June his left wing Vice-President, Henry Wallace, delivered a speech violently attacking the conduct of the Secretary of Commerce. The Secretary then retorted with an attack on Wallace. Roosevelt was extremely angry and upset at this unseemly exchange which so greatly pleased and entertained the Republicans and Conservatives. The quarrel occurred just four days after Roosevelt had suffered the worst defeat he had ever experienced in his dealings with Congress over social legislation. Congress, perturbed by the actions of American coal miners under their union leader, John L. Lewis, passed an anti-strike bill. Roosevelt who was very dependent upon the labour vote immediately vetoed it. But to his utter dismay conservative forces in the Congress were able to organise the two thirds majority necessary to over-ride his veto. Many who voted against the President were Democrats and the anti-Roosevelt press took great pleasure in mocking and denouncing Roosevelt as someone who could no more give leadership to his party than to the nation.

Over in England Churchill watched anxiously as his friend's setbacks continued. He remembered the last no-confidence debate in the House of Commons. He more than anyone could appreciate the President's position and also the determination with which Roosevelt refused to be rattled by the crises in Washington. He sent a message saying 'I have been so much distressed and angered to see the way you are being harried.

Knowing what war burdens are, I greatly admire the splendid calm and buoyancy with which you bear them amidst so much clatter'.[2]

The irritations in the President's life at this time were not all domestic. In foreign affairs there was, as always, de Gaulle. For by this summer of 1943 the jokes about the Bride had worn out, to be replaced by expressions of fierce anger as Roosevelt came to suspect de Gaulle of trying to undermine American control of French West Africa which had been gained in Operation TORCH. The President's usual laid back manner disappears as he bluntly tells Churchill, 'This is so serious that I should have to consider sending several regiments to Dakar and also naval vessels if there were any sign that de Gaulle proposes to take things over in French West Africa'. And a few days later the President explodes, 'I am fed up with de Gaulle and the secret *personal and political* machinations ... in the last few days indicates that there is no possibility of our working with de Gaulle'. Roosevelt's anger mounts, 'he is a very dangerous threat to us. I agree with you that he likes neither the British nor the Americans and he would doublecross both of us at the first opportunity'.[3]

At this time in the war Roosevelt also attempted a strong independent initiative towards the Soviet Union. He again proposed a meeting with Stalin. And without the presence of Churchill. As the American contribution of men and materials to the war effort came more and more to exceed that of any other member of the United Nations, including that of Britain, the President came to feel increasingly that American policy should not always be constrained by the alliance. He envisioned a conversation with Stalin that might be useful precisely because it did not have to include the leader of Britain and the British imperial system. But when Averell Harriman told Churchill of the President's intention, the Prime Minister was devastated. He felt a personal slight; he also felt politically threatened. For his exclusion would clearly damage his standing as a world leader and also his prestige within Britain. Despairingly he urged the President that not two, but all three leaders should meet. He suggested Scapa Flow, the British naval base in the Orkney Islands. 'I consider that a tripartite meeting at Scapa Flow or anywhere else on the globe that can be agreed not only of us three but also of the staffs, who will come together for the first time, would be one of the milestones of history. If this is lost, much is lost.'

The strength of feeling contained in this last short sentence shows itself again in the next paragraph as Churchill alludes explicitly to his friendship with the President as a justification for the urgency and directness with which he expresses his objection to Roosevelt's plan. 'You must excuse me expressing myself with all the frankness that our friendship and the gravity of the issue warrant.' And then keeping silent on the personal and political threat to himself he warns that a Roosevelt–Stalin meeting 'à deux' would be a gift to German propaganda. 'I do not underrate the use that enemy propaganda would make of a meeting between the heads of Soviet Russia and the United States at this juncture with the British Commonwealth and Empire excluded. It would be serious and vexatious and many would be bewildered and alarmed thereby.' But as in friendship generally it can happen that one partner depends more upon the relationship and is more ready to make concessions, so Churchill here, after making his case forcefully, finally agrees to go along with Roosevelt's decision. 'Nevertheless whatever you decide, I shall sustain to the best of my ability here.'

But, of course, Churchill was well aware that Roosevelt

needed to sustain him too. For though the rapidly enlarging American war effort began to make that of Britain look slight, Roosevelt and America still needed that effort. To be without it was unthinkable. The compulsions of political mutualities were a part of the friendship. Though determined not to be ruled by the ebullient Churchill, Roosevelt and his chief advisers were keen not to offend him or weaken his political position in Britain. But Roosevelt's approach to Stalin seriously tested these limits.

In the event, Stalin turned down Roosevelt's suggestion. The Soviet leader was intensely angered by the fact that the western allies would not initiate a second front in Europe until 1944. And his exchanges with the western leaders in the summer of 1943 were full of blame and bitterness. When the British and Americans captured Sicily and then invaded Italy and thus forced Hitler to divert troops from Russia to Italy, Stalin's appreciation was grudging.

For the western allies these successes in the Mediterranean theatre quickly presented a problem. For Mussolini's fascist government fell and the successor government under General Badoglio let it be known, in neutral capitals, that it wished to negotiate a surrender. Would Roosevelt's statement concerning Unconditional Surrender be adhered to? This was one of several urgent questions that prompted Roosevelt and Churchill to arrange another meeting. It was little more than two months since they had last met in Washington. But after the pause that followed operation TORCH the state of the war was now changing swiftly. The process of alliance needed direct face to face exchanges and reassurances.

This time Roosevelt and Churchill chose to meet in Canada, in Quebec City. King George VI arranged for them to have the use of the historic Citadel, a residence of his Governor General atop the Heights of Abraham which General Wolfe and his army had stormed nearly two centuries before and thus made Canada an entirely British possession. The Churchill–Roosevelt friendship progressed in one more place that was full of associations with the history of English-speaking settlement of North America.

As in his last departure from Britain Churchill sailed from the Clyde on the *Queen Mary* which had been repainted and looked less shabby than on that previous occasion. It seemed a sign of the improving state of the war. And so too did the fact that Churchill felt secure enough to include in his large party his wife Clementine and his pretty, twenty-year-old daughter Mary, the youngest of his four children. She had recently been commissioned second lieutenant in Britain's women's army, the Auxiliary Territorial Service, the ATS. Like Elliott Roosevelt on a previous occasion, she now formally served as her father's aide-de-camp.

The liner anchored in the naval dockyard at Halifax, Nova Scotia, where Churchill and his entourage of well over two hundred and thirty people boarded two special trains of the Canadian National Railway for the overnight trip through the moonlit lakes and dense forests of Eastern Canada to Quebec City. In the high citadel he quickly had his usual headquarters set up complete with map room. Many of his staff members were lodged at the Frontenac, a massive, green turreted castle-like hotel. From here the visitors could look down on the picturesque capital of French Canada, a walled city, founded around the time of the death of Shakespeare. Its narrow streets lined with old houses in the Norman style ran down steeply from Haute Ville dominated by the citadel to Basse Ville down by the broad St Lawrence River where ocean-going ships sailed by.

Churchill prepared to travel down to Hyde Park to which he had a second special invitation from the President. In Quebec where the August heat was considerable Churchill wondered how it would be all those many miles to the south. He asked the President whether we are 'right in thinking we should all bring our thinnest clothes?' Roosevelt wired back, 'Suggest thin clothes but be prepared for a variety of weather'. Then, perhaps remembering the peculiarities of Churchill's dress code, he added, 'Delighted to see you in any costume'.

Clementine was to have accompanied her husband on this visit but she had suffered badly from sea-sickness on the *Queen Mary* and Moran urged that she stay in Quebec City and rest. So Churchill set off with Mary and, after a wide detour to enable her to see Niagara Falls, they arrived at the Roosevelt home on the hot humid evening of 14 August. The following day they swam in the pool and then went to Mrs Roosevelt's cottage on the estate where they all had lunch in the open air. (The building of this cottage had been one of the ways of arranging a degree of separation within the Roosevelt marriage.) The American food, now of course familiar the world over, was exotic and intriguing to the British visitors accustomed both to rationing and a more staid cuisine. Outside Mrs Roosevelt's cottage in the wood on that hot day they ate hot dogs and hamburgers from the barbecue, corn on the cob, fish chowder and huge slices of water melon. The latter was especially acceptable in the intense heat. One night the heat and the humidity were such that Churchill just could not sleep. He got up, 'hardly able to breathe' and went outside and sat on a bluff overlooking the Hudson River until the sun rose.

The secret servicemen in khaki camouflage who patrolled the woodland on the President's estate were astonished to come upon the figure in the silk dressing gown with red and blue dragons studying the delicately whitening horizon.

But in every other way Churchill was content at Hyde Park. He felt welcomed and relaxed. One evening as he smoked his after-dinner cigar and drank his brandy he spoke at length of his hopes that the 'fraternal relationship' between Britain and the United States would continue in peace time. He even spoke of a common citizenship. It was a theme he would take up again on several occasions in the coming days and weeks. But Eleanor Roosevelt was made uneasy by the suggestion. As at Chequers a year or so before there was a moment of friction as she halted Winston's flow and suggested that his idea might imply an Anglo-American ganging up against other countries and thus weaken the concept, so important to her, of the United Nations. Churchill tactfully allowed this difficult moment to pass. And when he was on the train, travelling back to Quebec, he spoke of Mrs Roosevelt warmly, but, to some, not entirely sincerely as 'a spirit of steel and a heart of gold'.

The conference that then began in Quebec involved a lot of hard, intricate work of negotiation. And when it ended most of its chief participants were exhausted. Among the matters to be settled was the detailing of the military plans for the invasion of France in 1944. It was a miserable day for the British Chief of the Imperial General Staff, the Ulster-man Alan Brooke when he was told that he would not, as Churchill had once promised him, be in charge of this vast operation. The Supreme Commander, he was told, would be an American, General George Marshall. But in South East Asia the Supreme Commander, it was now settled, would be an Englishman, Admiral Louis Mountbatten. This very aristocratic figure would have as his deputy that rough talking American, General 'Vinegar Joe' Stilwell.

A commitment which Churchill argued strongly for at the conference was for a major military involvement in Italy. And Churchill and Roosevelt together reasserted their policy concerning Tube Alloys which in the months since Washington had once more been subverted by the President's subordinates. And, of course, there was still the problem of de Gaulle. At times the conference was a turmoil of conflicting advisers, staff officers, military egos, misunderstandings and suspicions. Hundreds of diplomats and senior officers in their Air Force, Navy and Army uniforms and with brief cases in their hands tramped to and from the Frontenac to the Citadel and back. Meetings went on through all the daylight hours on some subject at some level.

In the middle of the Quebec conference Roosevelt and Churchill decided to get away from it all and to spend some time in the country. They took with them Hopkins and Harriman and headed for the rural retreat of the Governor General, a large and well appointed log cabin beside a lake. Here they again spent a good deal of time fishing together. In the coming days fishing was to become an important shared pleasure. And they indulged in a good deal of traditional fishermen's banter. They also talked of other things. At their first lunch beside the beautiful tree-lined Grand Lac de l'Epaule, after they had eaten the little trout they caught, they discussed the state of the war in Asia. A leading question was what the next British initiative in that theatre should be. Churchill preferred an attack on Japanese-held Sumatra in Indonesia, at that time still the Dutch East Indies. Roosevelt was more in favour of a British campaign in Burma. Averell Harriman who dined with them remembered that 'The President used most of the glasses and salt cellars on the table making a V-shaped diagram to describe the Japanese position in the ... quadrant from

147

Western China to the South Pacific'.[4] Harriman thought that this attempt at strategic thinking 'was not too serious but a pleasant relaxation'. Harry Hopkins, having finished his white wine, fell asleep.

The following Monday morning the little party had to return to Quebec City for the hurly burly of the second plenary session of the conference. Much was discussed at this final meeting and though one shrewd British observer was of the opinion that 'I can't see what has been decided which takes us much beyond "Trident",' he also added, 'However I think much suspicion has been dissipated. They realise we are not bluffing on "Overlord" ...'[5] And indeed from this time on British scepticism about the invasion of France was formally set aside in favour of a commitment to the enterprise. As usual Churchill and Roosevelt ended the conference with a dinner party for themselves and those closest to them. It lasted until after half past one in the morning and even then Churchill was keen to keep going. As he continued to drink, he paced about the room prophesying eloquently what would happen in the various theatres of the war. Suddenly Harry Hopkins roused himself up from a slumped position at the table and said, 'Now I'll tell *you*, Mr PM what's going to happen'. Churchill came to a standstill, his jaw hung down questioningly. 'What is going to happen?' he asked. Harry Hopkins replied, 'Your pants is coming down'.

The following morning both leaders left Quebec City for a brief period of rest. Roosevelt went home to Hyde Park and Churchill went to a cabin deep in the maple woods on the Laurentian Mountains seventy miles from Quebec. Here he fished again and received sceptical messages from Roosevelt about his angling successes. 'I am delighted, as Quebec papers say, you are teasing the trout, but I do not believe New York newspaper accounts that you have landed a five pounder. I shall require sworn verification.' As proof of his achievements Churchill sent fish he had caught to Washington D.C. in the care of his daughter and aide-de-camp, Mary, who was to travel from Washington on to Ogelthorpe, Georgia, to pay a goodwill visit to a Women's Army Corps base.

On the first day of September Churchill and his wife, both feeling much better for their mountain holiday, arrived in Washington. Churchill stayed at the White House for some ten days. It was a suspenseful time in the matter of the surrender of Italy and of the recent Allied invasion of that country. Churchill said that 'I deliberately prolonged my stay in the United States in order to be in close contact with our American friends at this critical moment in Italian affairs. But the comedian Bob Hope made jokes about Churchill's pleasure in extended stays in America and even the staid Cadogan laughingly remarked, 'Winston will, I think, settle down in US'.

During his stay Churchill made some highly successful sorties from the White House. He was the invited guest at a meeting of the Washington Press Club where, as on a previous occasion, he made a strong and very favourable impression. He also travelled up to Boston to receive an honorary degree at Harvard University. Roosevelt took it upon himself to facilitate the necessary arrangements with the University President, Dr James B. Conant. (Churchill also received an accolade at a more popular level of American life. The hero of one of the hit films of 1943, the musical, *Girl Mad*, starring Micky Rooney and Judy Garland, is a young man who is witty, resourceful and above all, courageous in adversity. The writers gave him the name Churchill.)

The complexities and risks involved in the Italian situation placed an added stress on a weary Roosevelt and he decided to leave Washington for Hyde Park for another rest. With a singular gesture of generosity and confidence from one political leader to another, Roosevelt invited Churchill to stay on in his absence. As one of Churchill's advisers later remembered, the President said, 'Winston, please treat the White House as your home. Invite any one you like to any meals, and do not hesitate to summon any of my advisers with whom you wish to confer at any time you wish. Please break your journey to Halifax at Hyde Park and tell me all about it.'[6] Churchill accepted the invitation to stay on at the White House and did indeed convene and chair a meeting of senior allied officers for yet one more review of the rapidly changing war situation. It was an occasion of which Churchill was very proud. 'It was an honour to me,' he wrote, 'to preside over this conference of the Combined Chiefs of Staff and of American and British authorities in the Council Room of the White House and it seemed to be an event in Anglo-American history.'[7]

For one British observer that most unusual White House meeting over which Churchill presided was 'like a family gathering, and every sort of problem was discussed with complete frankness'. And he wondered whether, 'in all history, there has ever existed between the war leaders of two allied nations, a relationship so intimate as that revealed by this episode. The affection and trust which Churchill had inspired in Roosevelt was not the least of his services to the Allied cause.'[8]

An important item on the agenda of that White House meeting was the then uncertain outcome of the recent Allied landings in Italy and what Churchill called 'the fierce and critical battle for Naples'. The result of the fighting in that campaign was still very much a worry to him when he and his wife and daughter finally left Washington for Halifax, Nova Scotia, where they would embark for Britain. En route they stopped off at Hyde

Park to spend time with the President as he had requested. It was the Churchills' thirty-fifth wedding anniversary and everyone sought to forget the war and to have an enjoyable evening. After dinner Roosevelt made courtly speeches to them both and proposed their health. Then he insisted on driving them in his specially equipped car down to the small railway station close by from where they would continue their journey to the Canadian Maritimes.

Once on the train Churchill began a letter beginning, 'My Dear Franklin,' in which he dwelled at some length upon their relationship and its meaning for world history. Somewhat rhetorically he wrote, '... I cannot tell you what a pleasure it has been to me, to Clemmie and to Mary to receive your charming hospitality at the White House and at Hyde Park. You know how I treasure the friendship with which you have honoured me and how profoundly I feel that we might together do something really fine and lasting for our two countries and through them, for the fate of all.'

Some thirty-six hours after leaving Hyde Park Churchill's special train steamed into the naval dockyard at Halifax and there alongside the quay was the immense grey battle-cruiser, HMS *Renown*, its long dark guns standing out dramatically against the bright blue of the afternoon sky.

The voyage home had its dangers. Lieutenant Mary Churchill, making her way along the deck with a young officer during a violent storm was very nearly washed overboard. But in less than five days *Renown* anchored in the Clyde in an early autumn mist. Churchill was in excellent spirits.

But in Washington his friends Roosevelt and Harry Hopkins suffered yet another infuriating and disheartening blow.

Notes

1. Gilbert (quoting from Hansard), p. 428.
2. Kimball, p. 291.
3. Ibid., p. 285.
4. Harriman, p. 224.
5. Gilbert, p. 481.
6. Ibid., p. 501.
7. Churchill, Vol. 5, p. 138.
8. Ismay, p. 320.

8   Two's Company but ...

Menas: These three world sharers, these competitors.
William Shakespeare, *Antony and Cleopatra*,
Act II, Scene VII

After all the strains and confrontations of the Quebec Conference the ailing Harry Hopkins became totally exhausted and had to be admitted to Bethesda Naval Hospital near Washington, for a period of recuperation. One Sunday as he lay on his sickbed leafing through the newspapers, he was suddenly shocked and then outraged to see a huge coloured cartoon of himself in the conservative *Chicago Tribune*. Hopkins was, of course, hardened to criticism from the right wing press. But the viciousness of the cartoon and the accompanying article staggered even him. The drawing showed a leering Hopkins with the sinister Russian monk Rasputin looking over his shoulder. The article began:

> One evening in 1907, a tall, broad-shouldered peasant strode across the highly polished floor of the salon of Count Alexander Pavlovich Ignatiev ... He bowed clumsily to an ill assorted circle of nobles, politicians, schemers, charlatans, adventurers, clergy, and dignitaries ... Rasputin went on to sway Russia by the power of his eye. Nicholas, the czar of all the Russians fell on his knees before this curious mixture of penitent and debauchee and

called him a 'Christ' … For almost nine years this preacher of redemption thru sin virtually ruled Russia … His murder foreshadowed the end of the Romanoff dynasty and the collapse of the Russian empire in the World War.

The writer then proceeded to detail the similarities between Rasputin and Harry Hopkins. 'On a May day in 1933 a lean, gangly figure with thinning brown hair and dandruff made his way with his face twisted by a sardonic grin thru an ill assorted group of representatives, crackpots, senators, bums, governors, job seekers, political leaders, and toadies …' He continued: '… in the person of Harry Lloyd Hopkins, son of an Iowa harness maker, Santa Claus had come to town. He emptied his hands of other people's money. This strange and contradictory figure spent on and on to sway a nation and then the world. The President of the United States brought him into his official family and then into his private family and poured his innermost thoughts into the spender's prominent ears. The wife of the President adopted his small child in all but name …'[1]

Weak and feverish as he was Hopkins was incensed by these attacks and insinuations. He immediately wrote to a senior colleague in the Democratic Party, 'Can't you dig up some bright, young man in your office who will tell me that these bastards can be sued for libel?' But the reply, later endorsed by the President, was that as a prominent public figure Hopkins simply had to take it. Ironically these dark insinuations about Hopkins's peculiar personal and familial involvement with the Roosevelts came at the moment when his intimacy with them was decreasing. For it was about this time that he and his new wife Louise decided to cease living in the White House, which had been Hopkins's home for some three and a half years, and to rent a place of their own in Georgetown. Washington wits and gossip columnists would now no longer be able to refer to the White House as 'that 2-family flat'. But Roosevelt could be touchy. And it would seem that he resented this move to independence and the consequent loss of the close physical proximity of Hopkins. As his adviser began to make a home of their own for himself and his wife and daughter, Roosevelt's trust and confidence in him started to decrease.

In the weeks following the Quebec Conference there also developed a severe strain within Roosevelt's other friendship, that with Winston Churchill. The causes here though were political and military rather than personal. For while in that October Roosevelt worried about getting the gardener at Hyde Park to wrap up one of the estate's trees 'in burlap' 'and send it over by a bomber or otherwise in order to reach him (Churchill) at Chequers, England, before Christmas' – while the President troubled himself over such small matters of friendship, Churchill himself edged nearer and nearer to despair as he realised the growing divergence in British and American strategic thinking. It was the old story again. But now more painful. Churchill was still uneasy, panicky even, about OVERLORD, the plan to invade France. He remembered the Somme; he remembered Dunkirk. He was afraid that a failed invasion of Europe would revitalize Nazi Germany. He preferred as always to try and get at Germany from the South and the East, through Italy, the Aegean, the Black Sea and the Balkans. But American military commanders regarded such initiatives as a waste, bees in Winston's bonnet or perhaps ways of assisting his imperialist interests in the Eastern Mediterranean. The Americans believed that OVERLORD was the best and simplest way to deal with Hitler. This had been agreed on by both parties at Quebec and the deal should be stuck to. Accordingly British divisions and precious landing craft were sent back from Italy to Britain to be used in

OVERLORD. Churchill was horrified to see this happening at the very time the Germans were consolidating their position south of Rome and recapturing Greek islands which the British had taken but were denied the air support necessary to retain.

To the President Churchill wrote forebodingly, 'Hitherto, we have prospered wonderfully, but I now feel that the year 1944 is loaded with danger. Great differences may develop between us and we may take the wrong turning. Or, again, we may make compromises and fall between two stools. The only hope is the intimacy and friendship which has been established betweeen us and between our high staffs. If that were broken, I should despair of the immediate future.'[2]

Four days later he sends a message to the President with a still more urgent and more personal appeal. 'I have a great wish and need to see you. All our troubles and toils are so much easier to face when we are side by side.'

Roosevelt agreed to a meeting. But this proved more difficult to arrange than any of its predecessors. At long last Stalin had indicated a readiness to take part in the next meeting of Allied leaders. But Stalin was adamant that his need to stay in close contact with the now spectacularly victorious Soviet army prevented him from travelling any further than to the neighbouring country of Iran. He proposed Teheran, the Iranian capital, as the place for the meeting. Roosevelt argued strongly against this venue. Such a distant place would entail constitutional difficulties for him, he maintained. As President he was required to either sign or to veto bills from the Congress within ten days and if he were to go to such a remote part of the world, he might not be able to receive and return papers within the stipulated time. But Stalin insisted and insisted. And at last Roosevelt gave way and agreed to make the long journey to the Persian capital.

In terms of political symbolism this represented a kow-tow on the part of the President of the United States. It did too for Churchill who also agreed to go this great distance and who had already felt it necessary to go to Stalin in the Kremlin once before. Forty-five years on the Soviet Union would fall apart economically and politically. But in 1943 America and Britain were to a considerable extent the dependants of the militarily powerful and successful Soviet Union. The leaders of the two western countries had to go and try to secure its co-operation. They still depended upon Stalin not to make a separate peace with the Germans and also (and this was particularly important to the Americans) to come into the war against the Japanese once Germany was defeated.

The production of the atomic bomb, which was ultimately to be decisive in bringing about the Japanese surrender, still lay in the future. In late 1943 many senior American officers, Vinegar Joe Stilwell especially, believed that the Japanese would have to be pushed off the Asian mainland in a protracted land war. And in such a war not only the Soviets but the military forces of the Chinese republic headed by the Kuomintang leader, Generalissimo Chiang-Kai-shek, would be of great importance. Roosevelt was ready to entertain this view of the Pacific war and went along with those who urged that Chiang-Kai-shek should be invited to meet with him and Churchill at Cairo before the two western leaders continued their journey to Teheran to meet with Stalin.

The British, and Churchill especially, were greatly irritated by the participation of the Chinese leaders. Their objective at the Cairo meeting was to attempt yet again to settle the compelling claims of the Channel and Mediterranean campaigns and to agree upon a common policy to present to Stalin in Teheran. But Roosevelt and his advisers were in no mood to hear still more about

Churchill's ideas about Greece and the Balkans and the Black Sea and his anxieties about OVERLORD. As far as Europe was concerned the Americans wanted to stick to what had been agreed upon at Quebec and were, therefore, quite happy, even relieved, to devote a good portion of the Cairo conference to the Pacific and to the plans and concerns of Chiang-Kai-shek. So the Chinese Generalissimo, code-named Celestes, was summoned to Cairo and Churchill had to accept it. In Egypt which was then under British occupation, Churchill would be the host. He had, he told the President, made the arrangements for each of them to stay in a fine villa. And as for Celestes, he continued, making his attitude very clear, 'I have got the option on Tutankhamen's tomb'.[3]

Roosevelt set off on the first stage of his long journey to Stalin in the Presidential yacht *Potomac*. Then, as he had done when going to that first meeting with Churchill in Newfoundland, he transferred to a warship. This was the gleaming new battleship the USS *Iowa* which lay at anchor in Chesapeake Bay at the mouth of the Potomac. With her escort of three destroyers the *Iowa* set off on the cold, misty morning of 13 November with Oran on the coast of Algeria as her port of destination. On board the great ship Roosevelt's senior advisers worked long hours second-guessing the new objections to OVERLORD which the wily Churchill might devise.

In his specially fitted cabin the President started a diary of this long journey. And his sense of its importance in world history led him again to think, not altogether accurately, of other such journeys as related in the classical literature of Greece and Rome which he had studied at school. 'This will be another Odyssey,' he wrote, 'much further afield than the hardy Trojan whose name I used to take at Groton when I was competing for school prizes.' Roosevelt, like Churchill, had a sense of epic, and of himself as someone involved in an epic.

But the sense of epic soon turned to that of tragi-comedy. On the second day of the voyage there occurred one of the terrible absurdities of the Second World War. It began when the captain of the *Iowa* ordered an anti-aircraft drill. Roosevelt was wheeled from the luncheon table up on deck so that he might watch. Cotton wool was given to him to put in his ears as large coloured balloons, red, green and yellow, were floated up into the grey sky and the massive guns began firing on them, deafeningly. Suddenly, in a brief silence, Harry Hopkins heard an officer up on the bridge yelling, 'It's the real thing! It's the real thing!' Looking overboard Hopkins and his companions were astounded to see a torpedo streaking towards the *Iowa*. There was panic. The battleship abruptly altered course. Some of the ship's guns were trained on the torpedo which continued on its way, past the ship, at a distance of, in Hopkins's estimate, some six hundred yards.

The torpedo came not from a U-boat but from one of the escort destroyers which was engaged, not very expertly, in a practice. The torpedo had come close to sinking the President of the United States and most of the country's top military leaders. There were some twenty Army officers on board the battleship and the jokes about the Navy continued long after the *Iowa* had docked at Oran.

Here the President was greeted by General Eisenhower and his senior staff officers and again by his two sons, Elliott and Franklin Junior. Harry Hopkins's son Robert had also been summoned to join the family party. Then they all flew on to Cairo in the President's specially converted transport plane which came to be referred to as the Sacred Cow. Elliott Roosevelt was much impressed by the flight eastwards over the hundreds of miles of brown desert and then, suddenly and unexpectedly, over 'the greenest of green, so bright it makes you blink. This is the strip of rich earth running north and south, the thin ribbon of land irrigated by the Nile.' In another aircraft heading for Cairo at this time, the Ulster aristocrat, General Alan Brooke, also looked down in fascination on the desert. He could see 'the black bootlace of the tarmacked desert road,' which he had last seen during the campaign against Rommel when 'it was alive with lice-like lorries spaced out every hundred yards'. But now the war had moved on and the road was 'desolate and deserted without vestige of life to be seen on it'.[4]

The British delegation arrived in Cairo early enough for Churchill, suffering from a very heavy cold, to be present at the desert airport and, as host of the meeting, to welcome the President when the Sacred Cow landed. In Churchill's party was his daughter Sarah who wore the uniform of the Women's Auxiliary Air Force, the Waafs. Sarah, a stage and screen actress married to the middle-aged vaudevillian and comedian, Vic Oliver, was taking her turn to serve as her father's aide-de-camp.

Under heavy military escort the Prime Minister drove with his principal guest to the expensive and fashionable Cairo suburb where the conference was to take place. The actual meetings were held in Mena House, a palatial Arab building, which had once been the royal lodge of the Khedive Ismail who, under the Ottoman Empire had been the ruler of Egypt. More recently Mena House had been a luxury hotel. Roosevelt who had brought with him a domestic staff including waiters and his favourite Philippino cooks stayed in a villa with a stepped roof and a fine view of the nearby pyramids. Churchill and Chiang-Kai-shek each had a villa close by. Sarah Churchill found herself in an 'oriental-cum-Hollywood fantasy'. To her mother in November London she wrote, 'How lovely it is to wake each morning to this light gay

Friends' wives being friends. Eleanor Roosevelt and Clementine
Churchill broadcasting together at the Quebec Conference of 1944

Winston and Clementine cheered by troops on the *Queen Mary* as a tender takes the couple ashore on their return to Scotland

Stalin greets Churchill's daughter Sarah at Teheran. Behind the Prime Minister stands the Foreign Secretary, Anthony Eden and behind the President, Averell Harriman

Roosevelt meeting with Stalin without Churchill. One of Roosevelt's several attempts to 'get at' and have a special relationship with the Soviet leader

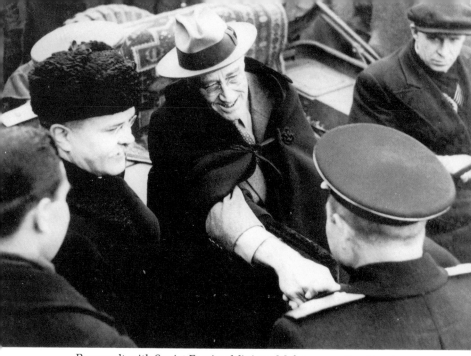

Roosevelt with Soviet Foreign Minister Molotov greeting Russian officers at Yalta

A friendship approaching its end. An ailing Roosevelt and a sceptical Churchill at Yalta

sunshine. Everything is too beautifully arranged and we live in palatial splendour and luxury. I don't know that I think Hollywood sets are exaggerated any more. The villas I have been to so far surpass anything I have seen – except on the films.' She went on, 'The security ... is so terrific that it is laughable – no matter where you turn, you come across a palsy of plain clothes detectives – Marines – Egyptian police – good old Cockney soldiers and carpet-slippered Abduls.'[5] The whole opulent suburb was cordoned off with barbed wire behind which were numerous machine-guns and anti-aircraft artillery. RAF Spitfires and Hurricanes constantly patrolled overhead. This was the milieu in which an American leader, a British leader and a Chinese leader met close to the pyramids in the ancient land of Egypt, to plan the renewing and the concluding of the present global war and the future planetary order.

On the day of the President's arrival Churchill had both lunch and dinner with him and was able, in some relief, to telegraph his Foreign Secretary, Anthony Eden, that 'All contacts with the President are favourable'. But when the first plenary session of the conference was held the following day he was not at all pleased to see how much time was devoted to China and the state of the war in the Pacific. An important presence in this and other meetings was the wife of Generalissimo Chiang-Kai-shek who served as her husband's interpreter. She and Churchill's attractive young daughter were the only women in this assembly. And Madame Chiang-Kai-shek was expert in attracting male attention to herself. Even the aloof Foreign Office mandarin Cadogan was provoked into noting how 'very smartly dressed' she was in her 'white jacket with a beautiful spray of rubies on it' and 'jade and pearl earrings'. And General Brooke sensing her strong political influence over her husband also reported how she exploited her sexual allure in that conference. He said that 'every small movement of hers arrested and pleased the eye'. He remembered how 'at one critical moment her closely clinging black dress of black satin with golden chrysanthemums displayed a slit which exposed one of the most shapely of legs. This caused a rustle amongst some of those attending the conference, and I even thought I heard a suppressed neigh come from a group of younger members.'[6]

But the British were not to continue to be fascinated by Madame Chiang-Kai-shek for long. Her presence and that of her husband clearly aggravated the disagreements and lack of sympathy between the British and American delegations. And yet within a deteriorating atmosphere in the conference generally the relationship between Roosevelt and Churchill grew still closer and warmer. It may well have been that the increase in personal cordiality was to each a compensation for political divisions.

One memorable example occurred after Churchill discovered that Roosevelt had never seen the Sphinx or the Pyramids. The Prime Minister immediately decided to do something about this. Of course if the President were to be taken to see these famous monuments, he would have to go by car. So in late afternoon, after the first plenary session was over Churchill and his daughter set off to find out how close a car could come to the monuments. When they discovered that it was possible for a car to come quite near to both the Sphinx and the Pyramids, father and daughter hurried back enthusiastically to invite the President to come sightseeing with them. Sarah noted how on this occasion her father's exuberance was an important feature of his relationship with the quieter Roosevelt. 'Such was my father's enthusiasm that the President leaned forward on the arms of his chair and seemed about to rise, when he remembered that he could not and sank back again. It was a painful moment. My father turned abruptly away and called over his shoulder: ''We'll wait for you in the car.'' Outside in the shimmering sun, I saw that his eyes were bright with tears. ''I love that man,' he said simply.'' '[7]

The President's bodyguard carried him to the car and the three of them set off in high spirits. Sarah remembered the trip to the Pyramids as 'a great success'. 'It was a lovely drive and the President was charming – simple and enthusiastic. I think he enjoyed himself – I think he appreciated the trouble Papa took. Papa loved showing them to him. It really is wonderful how they both get on – they really like and understand each other ...' Churchill himself also had a fond memory of this occasion when he and the President paused for a while by the Sphinx and 'gazed at her for some minutes in silence as the evening shadows fell'. It was one of those important occasions when the two relaxed in a deep wordless calm together, as they had done when staring out at the Atlas Mountains together a year before.

Thanksgiving Day dinner on 25 November was another happy time. The President hosted a meal for close friends and family members. He had had turkeys brought from the United States and they had been succulently roasted by the Philippino chefs. Propped up high in his chair the President carved the two birds in patriarchal fashion just as he did at Christmases at Hyde Park. As there were about twenty guests the carving took some time. And with his usual, quick feeling for his friend, Churchill worried that there would be none left for the host. 'As I watched the huge platefuls he distributed to the company I feared that he might be left with nothing at all. But he had calculated to a nicety, and I was relieved, when at last the two skeletons were removed, to see him set about his own share. Harry [Hopkins], who had noted my anxiety said, "We have ample reserves".'[8]

The white wine continued to flow as the pumpkin pie was served. An American army band played light music in the Glenn Miller style. And then came the brandy and the speeches which were, said Churchill, 'of warm and intimate friendship'.

And then the dancing began. Sarah Churchill the only woman at the party had to dance every dance, Elliott Roosevelt and Robert Hopkins being especially keen to take to the floor with her. Churchill grew fretful that there was no opportunity for him to dance. But at last he hit upon an idea. He downed his brandy and went and, ceremoniously, asked General 'Pa' Watson, the President's fat aide and jester, to dance with him. To Roosevelt's great amusement the two plump old men glided around in stately fashion to the strains of a romantic waltz. The couple then did the Tennessee Cakewalk.

The evening was a great success. Churchill concluded, 'I had never seen the President more gay'.

But among the senior advisers to the President and the Prime Minister the mood was less carefree. War weary and frustrated by divisions in their strategic thinking, these men, unmoved by the happy Thanksgiving dinner worked away at strategy meetings that became potentially ever more explosive. Vinegar Joe Stilwell remembered an especially bad moment involving the British General, Alan Brooke, Chief of the Imperial General Staff, and 'the tough guy', the American Admiral, Ernest J. King, Commander in Chief of the United States Fleet. Stilwell recalled, 'Brooke got nasty and King got good and sore. King almost climbed over the table at Brooke. God, he was mad! I wish he had socked him ...'[9]

The British Foreign Secretary arriving for the last days

of the Cairo meeting said, 'This Conference was among the most difficult I ever attended'. Anglo-American disagreements were painful and the timetable of meetings was poorly organised. Churchill, wrote Eden, regarded Roosevelt as 'a charming country gentleman'. But 'business methods were almost non-existent'. So Winston again 'had to play the role of courtier and seize opportunities as and when they arose'. Eden was painfully aware of how the presence of Generalissimo and Madame Chiang-Kai-shek highlighted Britain's disasters in the Pacific during the last two years and also her present weakness in that theatre. 'Our fortunes in the Far East were militarily at their lowest ebb. Singapore and our whole position in South-East Asia had been lost, Australia had been endangered. The contribution which we could make towards retrieving this situation was slight, and our American allies were impressed, almost to the point of obsession, with the merits of General and Mme Chiang-Kai-shek and their government. I sensed that even the future of Hong Kong was in question with them.'[10]

Himself very depressed about all this Eden was also struck by Churchill's patience and forbearance with the Americans and especially with Roosevelt as talk continued to centre on China and the Pacific War. 'Though the role of attendant listener was uncongenial to him, the Prime Minister played it faultlessly all these days, so that we came through without loss of any feathers, if not with our tails up.' But when the two delegations left Cairo and flew on, separately, to Iran to meet with Stalin the forbearance deteriorated. In Cairo the personal friendship easily transcended political tensions. In Teheran the friendship was more seriously threatened by political divisions than it had been for a long time.

Notes

1. Sherwood, p. 750.
2. Kimball, p. 565.
3. Ibid., p. 578.
4. Bryant, p. 73.
5. Sarah Churchill, *A Thread in the Tapestry* (André Deutsch, 1967), p. 61.
6. Bryant, p. 78.
7. Sarah Churchill, pp. 62–63.
8. Churchill, p. 341.
9. Bryant, p. 78.
10. Anthony Eden, *The Reckoning* (Cassell, 1965), p. 423.

9 Jealousy

The tribulations of our best friends arouse sentiments in us which are not entirely unpleasant.

La Rochefoucauld, *Maxims*

In that last week of November 1943 Roosevelt's party in 'Sacred Cow' and Churchill's in a York took off from Cairo and flew over the silver strip of the Suez Canal and then on over ancient landmarks from classical and Biblical wars such as the Dead Sea, the Tigris and the Euphrates. Teheran, despite its primitive water supply and sanitation, was in many ways a modern city; it was surrounded by desert and on the skyline were mountains where some of the American officers went hunting, bringing back tasty, tender venison.

Churchill had left Cairo in the khaki drill uniform of an Air Commodore and had changed into dress blue by the time he arrived in Teheran. 'His travelling wardrobe must be prodigious,' commented his flight companion, Anthony Eden, himself known as a dandy, who probably did not know how insistently Churchill's wife reproached her husband for wearing high-ranking uniforms on which he had no rightful claim.

When he arrived in Iran the Prime Minister was unwell and in a very bad mood. As a result of carousing and holding forth long into the small hours he had completely lost his voice. He grew angry at the poor security provided by the Iranians, when he was driven from the airport. And on that chilly, star-lit night in Teheran he found the British Legation with its floors of Arabian tiles too cold and cheerless. Churchill, Stalin and Roosevelt were to have dined together that first evening. But Sarah Churchill and Lord Moran persuaded a feverish, morose then sometimes querulous Churchill to go to bed. Finally he gruntingly agreed and surrounding himself with pillows and hot water bottles, dined in bed and then sipped brandy and read Dickens's *Oliver Twist* until midnight.

The following morning he awoke to discover that Roosevelt had been invited by the Russians, ostensibly for security reasons, to move into the Russian Embassy where the Conference was due to be held. Stalin had moved into lesser premises in the grounds of the compound in order to make room for the President. Roosevelt accepted the invitation and he and his party found themselves in the care of scores of Soviet secret policemen, all dressed in smart white coats, like servants, but with small arms bulging from their hip pockets.

Members of the British legation were sceptical about Stalin's act of courtesy and concern for the President's safety. 'Plainly,' wrote Moran, 'it is convenient for him to have the President under his eye where he cannot spend time plotting with the British Prime Minister'.[1] This initial physical distancing of Roosevelt and Churchill was to confirm and aggravate their political divisions and create, on Churchill's part, a sense of snub and hurt that were to continue intermittently throughout this conference in Iran.

That first full day Roosevelt and Stalin met together in the morning, without Churchill. They talked about China, problems of merchant shipping, de Gaulle (whom both heartily disliked) Indo-China, and a subject which, they agreed, could not be discussed in front of Churchill, India. The conversation went well. But it was a tête-à-tête that took place, an observer noticed, to Churchill's 'apparent chagrin'. Unquestionably Churchill was jealous, politically and personally. He told Harriman that he intended to 'get thoroughly drunk and be prepared to leave the next day'.[2]

After the first private conversation between Roosevelt and Stalin, there followed the first Plenary Meeting of the Conference. This was held in the great hall of the Russian Embassy. Some twenty delegates seated themselves on ornate mahogany chairs upholstered in striped silk, around a large, round oak table with a green baize cover. And here Churchill's sense of personal slight became part of a general British dissatisfaction with this tri-partite meeting. After Roosevelt, who was the only head of state present, had opened the conference with a brief introductory statement and then a review of the war in the Pacific, the occasion began to deteriorate. 'The President,' wrote Alan Brooke, 'then alluded to the Western Front and made a poor and not very helpful speech. From then onwards the conference went from bad to worse.' For some three and a half hours the three delegations sat around the large circular table in the lamplit hall of the Russian Embassy and listened to Stalin as he quietly but unrelentingly insisted on the launching of OVERLORD. 'During this meeting,' Brooke continued, 'and all the subsequent ones which we had with Stalin, I rapidly grew to appreciate the fact that he had a military brain of the very highest calibre. Never once in any of his statements did he make any strategic error … In this respect he stood out compared with his two colleagues.' Roosevelt was sympathetic to Stalin's demands concerning OVERLORD but Churchill, of course, was not. After the first plenary session had ended, his doctor encountered him and found him 'dispirited'. Moran departed from his prudent habit and asked him outright whether anything had gone wrong. He answered shortly: 'A bloody lot had gone wrong'.[3]

After the first session Roosevelt hosted a dinner in his quarters. Stalin was dressed more elaborately than he had been when Churchill last saw him in Moscow. He wore a brand new mustard coloured uniform with broad red stripes down the trousers and with immense gold epaulettes each bearing a large white star fastened with a red pin. Not to be outdone, Churchill again wore the dress uniform of a high-ranking RAF officer. Roosevelt in a tuxedo was amused by the two flamboyant uniforms on either side of him but was soon oppressed by the radical disagreements between his two guests. He found 'the diametrically opposed views of Stalin and Churchill a great barrier'.[4] Churchill himself grew increasingly dismayed as Roosevelt showed lack of solidarity with him in the tabletalk with Stalin. And the following day Churchill's sense of betrayal intensified when Roosevelt politely declined Churchill's invitation to lunch as a twosome prior to the second plenary session with Stalin. Roosevelt was keenly aware of being watched by the Russian secret police agents. He also genuinely wished Stalin to know that American foreign policy was not bound up with that of imperial Britain.

Churchill's resentment of Stalin deepened during the second plenary session. Stalin was often discourteous to Churchill on these occasions. Undoubtedly the Russian leader well remembered Churchill's passionate and energetic support at the end of the First World War for the White Russians who fought against the new Soviet regime. And though Stalin invariably deferred to Roosevelt, he was capable of speaking insultingly to

Churchill. The American naval chief, 'the tough guy', Admiral King, recalled how, in the second plenary session, 'It appeared that he [Stalin] liked to exasperate Mr Churchill and at one point in the meeting Mr Churchill became so angry that he got on his feet and told Stalin that he could not talk to him, or any other Britisher, in that manner, and proceeded to stump up and down the room for a few minutes until Mr Eden rose and spoke with him in a low tone, after which Mr Churchill resumed his seat and appeared somewhat calmer.'[5]

That night at the banquet hosted by Stalin matters grew worse. Throughout the dinner, reported Harriman, 'Stalin kept needling Churchill without mercy'. Why were the British so afraid of OVERLORD? Perhaps Churchill nursed some secret affection for the Germans? Perhaps he wanted to allow them a soft peace?[6] Everyone who remembered that evening, with all the heavy Russian food and the heavy drinking, recalled that Churchill for a long time accepted this teasing good-naturedly. He smiled and sipped his brandy whilst everyone else drank plentifully of the Russian champagne and vodka. But it would seem that Churchill who was still not in good health was holding his drink less well than usual that evening. For when Stalin offered yet one more toast, this one proposing the summary execution by firing squad of fifty thousand German war criminals, Churchill exploded with anger. Red in the face and neck he jumped to his feet. Any such policy, he shouted, was wholly contrary to the British sense of justice. The British people would never stand for such mass murder.

As Churchill raged on about the need for evidence and for proper legal trials, Stalin tried to keep a straight face but then laughed openly at the Prime Minister. Stalin then turned to Roosevelt and asked for his view of the matter. The President greatly relaxed by the champagne smiled at

Stalin and flippantly suggested that perhaps they could compromise on a figure of forty-nine thousand war criminals to be shot. Hurt came into Churchill's face. But then anger surged again when the President's son Elliott rose unsteadily to his feet and claimed that, along with other American soldiers, he had every sympathy with Stalin's proposal. Churchill, enraged by this young man's support for his mockers, strode from the room.

'At this intrusion,' the Prime Minister recalled, 'I got up and left the table, walking into the next room, which was in semi-darkness. I had not been there a minute before hands were clapped upon my shoulders from behind, and there was Stalin, with Molotov at his side, both grinning broadly, and eagerly declaring that they were only playing, and that nothing of a serious character had entered their heads. Stalin has a very captivating manner when he chooses to use it, and I never saw him do so to such an extent as at this moment. Although I was not then, and am not now fully convinced that all was chaff and there was no serious intent lurking behind, I consented to return, and the rest of the evening passed pleasantly.'[7]

But as for Elliott Roosevelt, who continued his military service in England, Churchill never received him again.

Not all Churchill's meetings with Stalin were difficult. On this very day when Churchill had twice risen up in anger, there had also been an occasion of remarkable harmony and unity among the three men. This was when Churchill presented to Stalin the great sword which King George VI had ordered made as a gift to honour the citizens of Stalingrad for the victory which was one of the greatest turning points in the war. The ceremony took place in the great hall of the Russian Embassy. The President sat in the centre of the room and Churchill and Stalin stood on either side of him. The sword was brought in, held aloft by a senior British officer. Twenty hefty British NCOs from the Buffs marched in with fixed bayonets and stood to one side of the large room. Then came a similar number of Russian soldiers bearing tommy-guns. A Russian army band played the 'Internationale' and then 'God Save the King'. After this Churchill presented the sword to Stalin for it to be sent on to Stalingrad. Churchill then made a brief speech in which he cited the inscription, in English and Russian, on the sword: 'To the steelhearted citizens of Stalingrad, the gift of King George VI, in token of the homage of the British people'. The sword was four feet long, fashioned in Sheffield of the finest tempered steel and chased with gold. The hilt was silver with leopard heads at the end. The scabbard was covered with scarlet lambskin with silver mounts.

Stalin received the sword with great ceremony, raised it aloft and dramatically kissed the hilt. He then took it to show President Roosevelt who pulled out the fifty inches of glittering tempered steel. The President was greatly impressed and moved by this instance of British ceremonial. Moist-eyed he read the inscription and murmured, 'Truly they had hearts of steel'.[8]

Stalin then handed the sword to his military adviser, Marshal Voroshilov, who spoiled the solemnity of the occasion by letting the sword slip out of its scabbard, strike him on the toe and fall with a clang to the floor. But then the Russian soldiers saved the situation by carefully taking up the sword and bearing it out of the room in a slow, formal march of great dignity.

The following day brought another of the happier occasions in Churchill's inevitably schizophrenic relationship with Stalin. This, the last day of November, was Churchill's sixty-ninth birthday and that evening he hosted a celebration dinner. Shortly after eight Roosevelt dressed in evening clothes and holding the beautiful, twelfth century Persian bowl which was his gift to Churchill was wheeled from the Soviet to the nearby British Embassy, an ornate white building flanked by a lily pond and guarded by turbaned Indian soldiers. Inside, Churchill and Stalin awaited him and were already in a jovial mood. The dining room was in the Persian style; the walls were entirely covered with a mosaic of small pieces of looking glass set at every conceivable angle. There were large, gilt-framed pictures of members of the British Royal Family and the Persian waiters were in red and blue liveries with white cotton gloves, the tips of the fingers of which hung limply and flapped about as the waiters handed the well heaped plates around. In Leningrad, the former and subsequent St Petersburg, the besieged embattled citizens starved. In Britain the food ration was meagre. But on this night in Teheran there was an abundance of food; boiled salmon trout from the Caspian Sea, cheese souffle, venison from the mountains of Iran, turkey and a large selection of French and Iranian wines. Stalin at first was disconcerted by the large amount of cutlery in his place setting but soon realised that he could eat, as was his habit, with but one knife.

As always on such occasions the drink flowed ever faster and Stalin and Churchill grew very boisterous. Stalin's interpreter, Pavlov, was kept very busy translating all the many toasts that were proposed. Diners would stand up and move around the table to touch glasses. At one point Churchill rose and raised his glass and said, 'I drink to the Proletarian masses'. And when all had done this, Stalin reciprocated with, 'I drink to the Conservative Party'. Churchill toasted Roosevelt 'as one who had devoted his life to the cause of the weak and the helpless, and one (and here Churchill glanced at Stalin) who through his courage and foresighted action in 1933 had indeed prevented a revolution in the United States ...'9

At the climax of the party when Churchill's birthday toast was about to be proposed, Stalin urged that Sarah Churchill and her brother Randolph who had just arrived in Teheran be invited in. Churchill was quite touched by the gesture. He wrote, 'I had not invited Randolph and Sarah to the dinner, though they came in while my birthday toast was being proposed, but now Stalin singled them out and greeted them most warmly, and of course the President knew them well'. Averell Harriman thought that 'Churchill's birthday dinner at the British legation surpassed all others in cordiality'. And Churchill himself felt that too. He wrote, 'I felt that there was a greater sense of solidarity and good-comradeship than we had ever reached before in the Grand Alliance ... I went to bed tired out but content, feeling sure that nothing but good had been done. It certainly was a happy birthday for me.'10

But for some, such as Ismay and Brooke it was the dessert that was the most vivid memory of that noisy birthday dinner that lasted until two o'clock in the morning. The desert was called Persian Lantern; it was an enormous piece of white icecream perched on a large block of ice in which there burned a candle. The waiter, bearing it aloft over the heads of the seated diners stopped to listen to one of Stalin's toasts that was being translated by Pavlov. The waiter did not notice that the icecream, so prettily illuminated, was rapidly melting. Suddenly the icecream slid off the ice and covered the unfortunate interpreter from head to foot. But not for one moment did Pavlov falter in his translating. It was the spirit of Stalingrad. When the translation was finally completed General Brooke sent for towels and wiped Pavlov down. 'To this day,' remembered Brooke, 'I can still see large lumps of white icecream sitting in his shoes and melting over the edges and through the lace holes.'11

The following day was the last day of the conference. Roosevelt awoke with the sense that despite all the good feeling of the previous evening, he had not really made that personal contact with Stalin, such as he had made with Churchill two years before and which, indeed, had been one of his chief objectives in making the long, long journey to Teheran. According to his Secretary of Labour, Frances Perkins, Roosevelt set out, in one last desperate effort to 'get to' Stalin by making mock of Churchill. It was one of the least pleasant occasions in the history of the Roosevelt–Churchill friendship. It is also an indication of how far the President was prepared to go to obtain Stalin's goodwill which he felt in such desperate need of. Frances Perkins reports that the President later told her:

'As soon as I sat down at the conference table, I began to tease Churchill about his Britishness, about John Bull, about his cigars, about his habits. It began to register with Stalin. Winston got red and scowled, and the more he did so, the more Stalin smiled. Finally Stalin broke out into a deep hearty guffaw, and for the first time in three days I saw light. I kept it up until Stalin was laughing with me, and it was then I called him "Uncle Joe". He would have thought me fresh the day before, but that day he laughed and came over and shook my hand.

From that time on our relations were personal, and Stalin himself indulged in occasional witticism. The ice was broken and we talked like men and brothers.'[12]

There is a suggestion here that Roosevelt is overstating and overestimating his new relationship with Stalin. Certainly subsequent history does not confirm that Stalin warmed to him either personally or politically after this episode in which Roosevelt's behaviour seems so demeaning and disloyal. Churchill comes out of it better. 'I must say,' reported Roosevelt, 'he behaved decently afterward.'

An important item of last business on that final day was the preparation of the communiqué. And this document which papered over the divisions that existed concerning present strategy and post-war political arrangements also rang with the rhetoric that Roosevelt employed in describing his relationship with Stalin. The communiqué ended with the words, 'We came here with hope and determination. We leave here friends in fact, in spirit and in purpose.'

Roosevelt and Churchill then returned to Cairo where the Prime Minister's health continued to deteriorate. His doctor observed, 'He is at the end of his tether. Teheran seems to have got him down. It is plain that he is riding for a fall.' But Churchill still laboured over his Balkans policy. He invited the Turkish President and Foreign Minister to Cairo and again tried to persuade them to enter the war and thus facilitate an eastern strategy for the Allies. To the relief and satisfaction of the Americans who wanted no such distraction from OVERLORD the two Turkish officials departed without in any way committing themselves. Roosevelt understood and could sympathise with their fear of both the Germans and the Russians and could see that 'these distinguished and amiable gentlemen would not want to be caught with their pants down'.

Another division between Churchill and Roosevelt on this second occasion in Cairo had to do with operation BUCCANEER. This was to be an amphibious attack on the Japanese on the Andaman Islands in the Bay of Bengal. Lord Louis Mountbatten was to be in command. Roosevelt regarded this project as an important part and indication of his commitment to Chiang-Kai-shek. He told Churchill, 'We had a moral obligation to do something for China.' Churchill argued that the cost of this operation in terms of shipping was excessive and potentially damaging to OVER-LORD. The meeting ended in complete deadlock between the two men. 'Thus we parted,' Churchill remembered, 'leaving Mr Roosevelt much distressed.'[13]

But as the President and his advisers came to realise the depth of Churchill's intransigence, and as they examined more closely the shipping issue, they came to doubt the feasibility of the proposed attack in the Bay of Bengal. A dispirited Roosevelt finally sent Churchill 'a laconic, private message' which read simply, 'Buccaneer is off'. The triumphant Prime Minister immediately telephoned the good news to Pug Ismay. Was Churchill referring to himself or to Roosevelt or to both, when, over the phone, he quoted to Ismay some words from *Proverbs* XVI:32, 'He that is slow to anger is better than the mighty; and he that ruleth his spirit than he that taketh a city'?[14]

BUCCANEER was off and suddenly the President wanted to be off too. There was no breach between him and Churchill. But Roosevelt appeared to have become weary after the days and days of negotiations. And many important issues remained unsolved. The future of Poland, for instance, so important to thousands of Polish American voters in that election year, had not been satisfactorily settled at Teheran. And the manner of policing the post-war world had still to be agreed upon. And though he felt pleased and relieved to think that he could deal with Stalin, that Stalin was in Roosevelt's word, 'get-at-able', he was disappointed and dejected about the abandonment of the initiatives that would have assisted the Chinese. Roosevelt was tired of it all and he suddenly wanted to go home, to be back home for Christmas. He ordered arrangements to be made swiftly for his departure. 'The President was off. No apologies – nothing,' wrote General Brooke irritably.[15]

The President flew westward and after several stops arrived in Dakar where the *Iowa* awaited him. On the voyage home he relaxed and recovered his spirits. But

Churchill, as he set out on the first leg of his journey home grew ever more ill. After he and his party had reached Tunisia he had pneumonia and then a heart attack. His condition was so bad that Sarah and his doctor had to prepare themselves to see him die.

Notes

1. Moran, p. 134.
2. Harriman, p. 265.
3. Moran, p. 135.
4. Elliott Roosevelt, p. 177.
5. Ernest J. King and Walter Muir Whitehead, *A Naval Record* (Cassell, 1953), p. 517.
6. Harriman, p. 273.
7. Churchill, p. 374.
8. Elliott Roosevelt, p. 182.
9. Sherwood, p. 792.
10. Churchill, pp. 387–8.
11. Bryant, p. 101
12. Frances Perkins, *The Roosevelt I Knew* (New York, 1946), p. 173.
13. Churchill, p. 410.
14. Ismay, p. 342.
15. Bryant, p. 104.

10   In the Time of Overlord

Interiorly, most people enjoy the inferiority of their best friends.
Lord Chesterfield, *Letters*, 9 July 1750.

When Churchill flew from Egypt to Tunisia his York aircraft landed at the wrong airport. His host, General Eisenhower, was waiting for him at an airport some forty miles away. While Churchill, surrounded by his despatch boxes sat disconsolately on that desert airstrip and shivered in the chill dawn air and waited for things to be sorted out, he looked, to one observer, General Brooke, more ill, more pale, more dispirited than he had ever looked before. Brooke later described how 'they took him out of the plane and he sat on his suit case in a very cold morning wind, looking like nothing on earth. We were there about an hour before we moved on and he was chilled through by then.'

Churchill was eventually put back on the plane and a ten minute flight brought him to the airbase where Einsenhower and other senior American officers awaited him. In the General's official car on the journey to Eisenhower's headquarters, a large villa known as the White House or La Maison Blanche near Carthage, Churchill came near to breaking down. Falteringly he managed to say to Eisenhower, 'I shall have to stay with you longer than I had planned. I am completely at the end of my tether ... I cannot go on until I have recovered some strength.'[1]

The following day Churchill had a very high temperature. A portable X-ray machine was rushed from the American base at Tunis. The device revealed a shadow on the lung. The army doctors diagnosed pneumonia and feared pleurisy. Yet, despite his high fever and his, for him, unprecedented weakness, he still struggled to work and to take urgent decisions. Harold Macmillan and Desmond Morton were ordered over from the British Mission in Algiers. The Prime Minister's son Randolph also arrived. And Clementine flew in from London. When he was forced to admit that he was incapable of working, Churchill asked to have a novel read aloud to him. Jane Austen's *Pride and Prejudice* was his choice and his youngest daughter, Mary, the volunteer reader.

Over in Washington the President, along with Harry Hopkins, was intensely worried about his friend's critical condition but still sought to be light-hearted in his response to the bad news. 'I am distressed about the pneumonia and both Harry and I plead with you to be good and throw it off rapidly ... *The Bible* says you must do what Moran orders but at this moment I cannot put my finger on the verse and chapter.'[2]

Along with pneumonia Churchill also suffered a slight heart attack. He grew weaker. For some six days his life hung in the balance. But then, very slowly, he started to recover. Immediately he threw himself back into his political work. He was particularly concerned that a proposed Allied landing further up the Italian coast at Anzio should take place. But there were many among the President's military advisers who doubted the usefulness of such an enterprise as indeed they doubted that of the entire campaign in Italy.

While Churchill planned and pushed this particular project, he had to accept that he was still sufficiently ill that he would have to remain in Tunisia over Christmas. And this was the reason he did not receive his Christmas presents from Roosevelt. Again the President had sent to Chequers a Christmas tree from Hyde Park and also an attractive case of maps of various regions of the world assembled by the National Geographic Society. A third gift was a copy of a volume of Roosevelt's speeches, *Addresses of the President*. The inscription recalled that important moment of their coming together in the days immediately after Pearl Harbor. It read, 'To Winston S. Churchill. In Memory of having him in the White House for Christmas 1941.' Another and very special gesture by the President was his action in making available to Churchill, during the convalescence the doctors insisted on, the villa at Marrakech which the two of them had visited together after the Casablanca Conference. It was within a convenient flying distance from Tunisia and, of course, it had special memories for both men. They had got into the habit of referring to it, because of the beautiful vegetation that surrounded it, as Flower Villa. Here a still very weak Churchill, finding it difficult to walk, arrived on the day after Boxing Day. He later told the President, 'I am indeed in the lap of luxury thanks to overflowing American hospitality'. Roosevelt hoped that his friend would have a complete rest and even do some painting. 'I am delighted that you are really so much better,' he telegraphed, 'And I wish I could be with you at the flower villa at Marrakech. I hope you have sent for your brushes.' But sadly Churchill had to reply, 'I am not strong enough to paint.' He spent a good deal of his time listening to Gilbert and Sullivan's *Pirates of Penzance* and *Patience* on records which his daughter Mary had bought for him at Christmas.

Churchill remained at Marrakech for some two and a half weeks. During this time he would have conferences with Eisenhower, Montgomery, the Czech President, Eduard Benes, and with generals involved in the detailed planning of the Anzio landings. He had a meeting with General de Gaulle; it began frostily but grew more cordial as the lunch proceeded. He also took time to relax. He played cards a great deal with Max Beaverbrook whom he had invited over from Britain. And along with his wife and members of his family he enjoyed daily picnics in the Atlas Mountains. His health improved. But unquestionably the greatest boost to his morale and his health at this time occurred when he learned that the President had decided to support the proposed landing at Anzio thirty miles south of Rome. For Churchill this was both a political and a personal success. Responding to the President he exclaimed, 'I thank God for this fine decision which engages us once again in whole-hearted unity upon a great enterprise.' He later went on to say, 'The sun is shining today, but nothing did me the same good as your telegram showing how easily our minds work together on the grimly simple issues of this vast war.'[3]

Churchill, still not completely recovered from his illness, left Marrakech 14 January, 1944. He flew to Gibraltar and there boarded the battleship *King George V* for the voyage to England. He confessed to the President that he was still 'rather shaky on my pins', but thanked him for intervening to arrange for his convalescence. 'I must thank you for the delightful stay we had at Flower Villa and for the princely hospitality which you extended to me through the American Army.'

Churchill was not alone in being shaky on his pins; both leaders of the western alliance were now in the grip of illness. Around New Year's Day 1944, Roosevelt came down with what he told Churchill was 'a mild case of the "flu" which in a mild form has become epidemic throughout the country'. It kept him in bed for some days. But Roosevelt insisted that it was not important. Attempting one of his WASP jokes, he told Churchill, 'This epidemic is very widespread but while it is not serious it makes you feel the way an Italian soldier looks'. But in the event this supposedly 'mild' illness proved to be the prelude to a major and accelerating deterioration in the President's health during 1944. Early that year doctors discovered that Roosevelt was suffering from acute hypertension and congestive heart failure. The doctors prescribed digitalis and persuaded him to take radical steps to reduce his weight.

During the first half of 1944 the vast and complex preparations for D-Day were the centrepiece of the Allied war effort. And politically these were headed by two elderly, sick men. There finally came a point when Roosevelt had to accept his doctors' advice that he leave Washington for a month's rest and recuperation. He went to stay on a plantation in South Carolina owned by one of his economic advisers, Bernard Baruch, Churchill's long-time friend and financial adviser. Whilst in Southern Carolina the President employed the conservative Admiral Leahy in the role of political consultant that had formerly been performed by the now ailing Harry Hopkins who had been out of Roosevelt's favour for some time. Whilst the President was not actively directing the government in Washington Churchill was acutely sensitive to the more bureaucratic reception his messages met. Always in their exchanges there had been a difference between their personal and individual styles on the one hand and the style of those portions of their messages drafted by their advisers on the other. From Washington at this time the latter predominated. For instance, during the months before the invasion of Normandy Churchill continued to fret about the transfer of men and materials from the Italian Front. But the responses to him from Washington were bluntly unconciliatory. General Brooke spoke about 'the President's unpleasant attitude lately'. But Churchill claimed to see through these replies. 'I cannot believe any of these telegrams are from the President. They are merely put before him when he is fatigued and pushed upon us by those who are pulling him about.'[4]

But for Churchill such tensions with Washington were trivial compared with his larger anxiety and stress with regard to D-Day. He was terrified that it might be a failure and the invading troops pushed back into the sea. As the day grew closer Churchill grew increasingly over-wrought. And his emotional state greatly worried those around him. 'PM I fear, is breaking down,' noted Cadogan after a meeting of the War Cabinet in mid April 1944. And General Brooke recollected how in a moment of misery and despair Churchill 'said Roosevelt was not well and he (himself) was no longer the man he had been.' Shocked at Churchill's state Brooke added, 'I have never yet heard him admit that he was beginning to fail'.

During these days of intense and mounting tension the President, for all his own ill health, performed several acts of kindness to help and sustain Churchill. The President sent him a recent portrait of himself, a gesture to which Churchill responded quickly and enthusiastically in kind. 'My dear Franklin, You kindly sent me recently a portrait of yourself which I like very much and have hung in my bedroom. Here is a tit for tat. I hope you will accept it, flattering though it be to me, and like it as much as I do yours.'

Around this time they also shared a literary and linguistic interest together which gave the President an opportunity for some laid back flattery. The subject was Basic English. This was a radically compressed and simplified version of the language with a minimal vocabulary of eight hundred and fifty words including only eighteen verbs. It had been developed by C.K. Ogden who did research in linguistics at Cambridge in collaboration with the literary theorist I.A. Richards. Churchill envisioning a post-war world in which the English-speaking peoples would be a major force was keen to promote Basic English as an easily mastered communications device for the whole world. He told Roosevelt, 'My conviction is that Basic English will prove to be a great boon to mankind in the future.' The President replied that 'we are interested'. But in a way that gently and skilfully implied his admiration for Churchill's literary and rhetorical powers he also speculated on how Churchill's famous 1940 speech about offering 'blood, sweat, toil and tears' would have fared, if it had had to be translated into Basic English. 'Incidentally I wonder what the course of history would have been if in May 1940 you had been able to offer the British people only "blood, work, eyewater and facewater", which I understand is the best that Basic English can do with five famous words'.[5]

On D-Day itself there came another gesture from Roosevelt. Churchill had been greatly taken with the elegance of the typeface in a letter sent to him by one of the generals in the Pentagon. On the day the greatest invasion in history was set in motion the President sent to Churchill two electric typewriters with the typefaces he so admired. He told Churchill that he hoped he would accept them 'as a gift from me and as a symbol of the strong bond between the people of America and Great Britain'. Churchill was delighted both by the gifts and the sentiments they were intended to convey. His thank you note was typed on one of the machines.

As the D-Day landings proved successful and the

invasion of France gathered momentum, Roosevelt, despite his ill health set about obtaining the Democratic nomination for the presidential election in November of 1944. Clearly, given his physical condition this was most unwise. But along with his ingrained commitment to public duty and service he had a strong sense of his indispensability as America's war leader. Also he and senior members of his party were in no doubt that without Roosevelt heading the ticket the Democratic Party might well be heavily defeated. As part of his campaign he decided to show himself giving leadership in the war in the Pacific. On the evening of 14 July he and his party left Washington and spent most of the next day at the home of his former lover, Lucy Mercer Rutherford on her estate in New Jersey. Then he went on a brief visit to Chicago where the Democratic Convention was being held. He was evasive about his preference for his Vice-Presidential running mate but finally acquiesced in the nomination of Senator Harry S. Truman of Missouri. Roosevelt continued his journey to California and embarked at San Diego in the heavy cruiser USS *Baltimore* and sailed for Pearl Harbor. Here he conferred with General MacArthur and Admiral Nimitz and assisted them in the negotiating of strategic issues in the Pacific. As Admiral King observed, 'the timing suggested that the President' in this election year, 'wished to emphasise his role as Commander in Chief of the Army and the Navy'.[6] He returned to America via Alaska and the state of Washington where at the naval dockyard at Bremerton he delivered a speech which for many members of the press and audience demonstrated shockingly the extent of his ill health.

Churchill also went on his travels. He visited British troops in Italy, and from a greater and safer distance than he would have wished he observed the Allied landings on

the south coast of France which were codenamed
DRAGOON. This was the very initiative which he had
resisted for so long, hoping instead for an Allied strike
into the Balkans. Churchill also paid visits, as the ailing
President would have liked, to various places in recently
liberated Normandy. In the aftermath of D-Day
Churchill's immense relief at its success was clear to
everyone around him. But he still worried about the
Mediterranean campaign. He could not accept the
American view that it was a theatre of secondary
importance. Churchill had hopes of pushing further and
faster into Northern Italy and then into Northwestern
Yugoslavia and Austria and Hungary. He talked of
liberating Vienna and Prague, perhaps even Budapest
before the Russians did. He was much more sceptical,
indeed fearful about Soviet intentions in this area of
Europe than were Roosevelt and his advisers. The
President pleaded, insisted that there be no change in
military objectives. 'My dear friend, I beg you to let us go
ahead with our plan.' It was, after all, election year in
America and the President felt it necessary to tell
Churchill that 'for purely political considerations over
here I would never survive even a slight setback in
OVERLORD if it were known that fairly large forces had
been directed to the Balkans'.[7]

Churchill grew concerned about the wide divergence of
view on this and other matters. He saw it, as usual, as a
result of the activities of the President's and his own
subordinates. Once again he stressed the power of their
personal relationship. 'Why is all this effective direction to
be broken up into a committee of mediocre officials such
as we are littering about the world? Why can you and I
not keep this in our own hands, considering how we see
eye to eye about so much of it?'[8] Churchill also began to
agitate for another get together. 'When are we going to

meet and where? That we must meet soon is certain.' And just a few days later he persists, 'There are several serious matters in the military sphere which must be adjusted between our staffs. I ... would greatly welcome a few frank talks with you on matters it is difficult to put on paper.' Several venues were proposed by Churchill including Scotland and Bermuda but none proved acceptable until it was suggested that they might return to Quebec City. When the President agreed to this, Churchill was delighted. 'I am looking forward immensely to seeing you again and trying to clear up with you in the light of our friendship some of the difficulties which beset even the path of dazzling victory.'

As the time for the meeting approached Roosevelt again sought to establish a good mood and atmosphere by sending gifts as tokens of reassurance and personal affection. He sent Churchill some documents to do with the history of the Royal Navy and some others that formed part of the long genealogy of the Churchill family. The Prime Minister responded with a 'My Dear Franklin' letter thanking him for 'the naval signatures and the papers on the early Churchills'. As he himself prepared to sail to Quebec City he made arrangements to send to the President who was so interested in naval engineering, the original model of the prefabricated harbour which the British had towed over the Channel to Arromanches in order to land more troops after the initial landings on the beaches. Two weeks before he set off for Canada Churchill was concluding his tour of Italy. And from there he wrote to his wife Clementine, confiding in her about the importance of the coming meeting with Roosevelt. He told her, 'This visit of mine to the President ... is the most necessary one that I have ever made since the beginning, as it is there that various differences that exist between the Staffs, and also between me and the American Chief of Staff must be brought to a decision.' And such resolving of differences, he went on, hinged entirely on the personal relationship. 'These are delicate and serious matters to be handled between friends in careful and patient personal discussion.' One of these matters was the need of a financially exhausted Britain for a new Lend Lease commitment from the Americans after the war had been won in Europe.

On the morning of 5 September, 1944 Churchill with his wife and staff boarded his special train and travelled to Greenock in Scotland where they once more boarded the liner, *Queen Mary*. There were some four thousand other passengers on the ship, mostly American soldiers who were either wounded or returning home on leave. When Churchill learnt that the ship had been waiting for him and that the GIs had lost some of their leave he immediately cabled Roosevelt asking that it be made up to them; the President readily granted the request. That first night on board Churchill's party dined on oysters and champagne and other luxuries. Churchill talked about the coming break-up, as victory approached, of his coalition with the Labour Party and the tactics these present partners and future opponents would employ. He was in lively form. But the following day as the ship sailed into the heat and humidity of the Gulf Stream, he grew dispirited and bad-tempered. The weather along with the anti-malaria tablets he had to continue to take following his trip to Italy had a strong and debilitating effect upon him. As the voyage continued he grew increasingly depressed. 'He is very flat,' observed one of his party and, remarked another, 'in his worst mood'.

But when, after a voyage of four and half days the *Queen Mary* arrived in the harbour of Halifax, Nova Scotia, and the Prime Minister went ashore, his spirits revived markedly. He was received by a number of soberly dressed Canadian dignitaries surrounded by Mounties wearing their scarlet tunics and full regalia. From the observation platform of his Canadian National Railways train he enjoyed the enthusiastic greeting of a large crowd of Maritimers and joined with them in singing Canada's two national anthems, 'God Save the King' and 'O Canada'.

A twenty-hour rail journey brought the party to Quebec City, where Roosevelt, a guest in Canada, had made a special point of arriving ten minutes early. It was a gesture of high courtesy. The meeting of the Roosevelts and Churchills was, as one onlooker, Pug Ismay, remembered, 'more like the reunion of a happy family starting on holiday than the gathering of sedate Allied war leaders for an important conference'. But the British were horrified at the marked deterioration in the President's health and appearance. One of them was shocked to have to report, 'I heard him say nothing impressive and his eyes seemed glazed'.[9] Pug Ismay was appalled at the President's physical condition. Ismay had last seen Roosevelt at the Cairo meeting and before that, on the well remembered occasion in Washington when Churchill had been informed of the fall of Tobruk. Arriving at the second Quebec Conference Ismay was staggered to see how Roosevelt looked. 'I was shocked to see the great change that had taken place in the President's physical appearance since the Cairo Conference. He seemed to have shrunk; his coat sagged over his broad shoulders, and his collar looked several sizes too big. What a difference from the first time I had set eyes on him less than two and a half years ago ... on 'Tobruk morning' he had looked the picture of health and vitality.'[10] And Churchill's doctor, Lord Moran, surmised more serious implications in the President's appearance. 'At Quebec he seemed to me to have lost a couple of stone in weight – you could put your fist between his neck and his collar – and I said to myself then that men at his time of life do not go thin all of a sudden for nothing.' And like Roosevelt's critics in the United States, but without their hostile motives, Moran questioned whether the President's obvious ill health affected his political abilities. '... I wonder how far Roosevelt's health impaired his judgement and sapped his resolve to get to the bottom of each problem before it came up for discussion.'[11]

And certainly feelings of good natured bonhomie based on securely established friendship rather than political acuteness and alertness seem to have characterised the meetings between the President and Prime Minister on this second visit to Quebec City. Such easygoingness prompted by their ill health and war weariness helps explain, for instance, the commitment both made, and later regretted, to the so-called Morgenthau Plan. This was a policy that had been developed by Roosevelt's Secretary of the Treasury, Henry Morgenthau; it proposed that after the Allied victory Germany be deprived of all its industrial potential and converted into a pastoral state. This, the argument ran, would help make Britain more competitive after the war and also prevent Germany from re-arming in the future. Initially Churchill had doubts but, persuaded by his chief scientific adviser, Lord Cherwell, 'the Prof', he agreed to the proposal. President and Prime Minister both initialled the policy document without thinking through the downside of such a reorganisation of western Europe. The professional diplomat Cadogan became frustrated as he listened to the self indulgent and disorganised conversations between the two political leaders. In his diary he noted, 'PM, Pres and at times Morgenthau and Cherwell, talked – or rambled – on a variety of things.' 'It's quite impossible to do business this way,' complained Cadogan irritably. 'Towards the end of lunch ... Pres and

PM rambled hopelessly. I tried to pin them down to the point, but they always wandered away. Lunch went on till 4.'[12]

But Churchill and Roosevelt were soothed and relaxed by their lunchtime rambling together. There seem to have been no disagreements; Churchill was especially pleased to find that the President was in favour of the continuance of the campaign in Italy. 'There is to be no weakening of Alexander's army,' he telegraphed triumphantly to the War Cabinet in London. Another occasion of feeling good together occurred on the afternoon of the final day of the Conference when Prime Minister and President were awarded honorary degrees by McGill University. Because of the President's physical difficulties the academic dignitaries travelled from Montreal up to Quebec City for the ceremony. In his acceptance speech Churchill was more explicit than usual about his friendship with Roosevelt. As the ailing President looked on, visibly moved, Churchill recalled the development of the friendship which he saw as having been forged 'under the hammer blows of war'. He went on, 'And the fact that we have worked so long together, and the fact that we have got to know each other so well under the hard stresses of war make the solution of problems so much simpler, so swift and so easy it is.'[13]

When the bustle of the Conference in and around the Citadel ended, the private element in the relationship between the two men was again emphasised by Roosevelt's invitation to Churchill and to the members of his family accompanying him to come and stay at Hyde Park. Roosevelt had, of course, done the same thing after the first Quebec meeting. During Churchill's second stay in the President's home an important conversation between the two men had to do with the atom bomb. They reconfirmed British and American co-operation in the research and manufacture but they also agreed not to make any public announcement as yet concerning the state of the project. But most of the shared time at Hyde Park was spent in relaxation together, in outings and picnics in the fine autumn weather of upstate New York that year. But then, sadly, for both men, came the time to part. To Churchill the quiet of the President's country estate was replaced by the razzmatazz surrounding a world figure on the move. One of Churchill's secretaries, Marian Holmes, recalled their flamboyant departure. 'Leaving Hyde Park was an experience. The PM sat with the President in his car which was surrounded by Cadillac autos full of bodyguards and G-men. When we drove through Poughkeepsie, they jumped on the running boards and made a terrific show. All traffic on the roads was brought to a standstill by order of the State Police ...'[14] From Poughkeepsie the Churchill party took an overnight train to New York City where the *Queen Mary* was docked, awaiting them. On the return voyage Churchill was in an altogether different mood from that in which he had sailed from Britain. 'Winston seems in better heart,' observed Moran and a senior naval adviser noted simply, 'PM in excellent form'. The trip had had a political purpose. But like the others it was the closest Churchill ever came to a holiday during more than five years of war. The rest, the trip, the pleasurable conversations with Roosevelt had relaxed and renewed him.

They would not meet again for more than four months when they came together on the island of Malta prior to travelling on to meet with Stalin at the resort town of Yalta in the Crimea. By that time new and painful tensions, some of the worst ever, would have affected the friendship between Churchill and Roosevelt. But as he sailed back across the Atlantic in the *Queen Mary* Churchill sensed that his relationship with the President had reached one of its high points. In sending a report of this meeting to the Prime Minister of Australia Churchill described it as 'a blaze of friendship and unity'.

Notes

1. Gilbert, p. 603.
2. Kimball, p. 621.
3. Gilbert, p. 630.
4. Ibid., p. 700.
5. Kimball, Vol. III, p. 154.
6. King, p. 567.
7. Kimball, p. 223.
8. Gilbert, p. 805.
9. John Colville, *The Fringes of Power: Downing Street Diaries 1939–1955* (Hodder and Stoughton, 1985), p. 514.
10. Ismay, p. 373.
11. Moran, p. 179.
12. Alexander Cadogan, *The Diaries of Sir Alexander Cadogan O.M. 1938–1945*, ed. David Dilks (Cassell, 1971) p. 665.
13. Gilbert, p. 968.
14. Ibid., p. 970.

11 Coda

Roosevelt also returned home with some of his energy restored to him. And he immediately applied it to his campaign to defeat his Republican opponent, Thomas E. Dewey, the Governor of New York. One of Roosevelt's assets in the campaign was the motion picture *Wilson*.

The movie had been produced by Darryl F. Zanuck and other Roosevelt sympathisers and backers in Hollywood. A film biography, the picture showed how in 1918 America had won the war but begun to lose the peace due to lack of Republican co-operation with the ailing President, Woodrow Wilson, in the matters of the peace treaty and the creation of the League of Nations. The similarity between the opportunity available in 1919 and that available in 1944 with Roosevelt's commitment to the founding of a United Nations Organisation at the end of the war was made menacingly clear. Roosevelt presented Churchill with a print of the film which the Prime Minister watched on his journey home on board the *Queen Mary* which was again serving as a troopship for American soldiers. The Prime Minister could not conceal his sense of the propaganda element in the film; at the same time he made it clear that he approved of the film just as he hoped, again, for a Roosevelt victory in the election. From the liner he messaged the President, 'We all saw Wilson's film with great interest and pleasure. It made a strong impression upon American officers and troops, but some comments were made about it being effective Democratic Party propaganda. My feeling is that it can do nothing but good to common cause.'[1]

Just four days after saying goodbye to Churchill Roosevelt made one of his liveliest and best remembered campaign speeches at a rally in the Statler Hotel in Washington. The Republicans who regularly made attacks on the President's wife, daughter and sons, now targeted the President's dog Fala, who, they claimed, basked in luxury at the public expense. They accused the President of wasting taxpayers' money by sending a Navy cruiser to fetch Fala, after the President had absentmindedly left him behind in Alaska after his recent visit there. With mocking wit the President defended his dog against such character assassination. Fala was a Scottie and, Roosevelt insisted, 'Scotch in his soul'. He simply would not tolerate such waste. The Democratic audience delighted in the President's continuing humour as he deflected the criticism. And over in England Churchill, though as always 'off the record' when commenting on American domestic matters, also took much pleasure in his friend's rhetorical success. He cabled briefly, 'Off the record – I have read your speech with much gusto and delighted to see you in such vigorous form.'[2]

But Churchill was less pleased to hear of Roosevelt going into New York, Dewey's state as well as his own, to campaign for hours from an open car in the cold, heavy rain. There could be something grandmotherly in the way these two elderly men nagged each other about neglecting their health. 'I was delighted to see the proofs of your robust vigour in New York,' began Churchill. 'Nevertheless I cannot believe that four hours in an open car and pouring rain with a temperature of 40 and clothes wet through conform to those limits of prudence which you would be so ready to describe if it were my case. I earnestly hope you are none the worse and shall be grateful for reassurance.'

But Roosevelt loftily dismissed such worries with his old confidence and self-regardingness. He replied, 'My journey to New York was useful and rain does not bother an old sailor. Thank you for your advice nevertheless.' By the time Churchill read this, the President had moved his campaign on to Massachusetts where, in Boston, he had another successful grand rally. The ageing Roosevelt was being assisted by some of the rising young stars in show business. The twenty-six-year-old Frank Sinatra was the singer of 'America' at the Boston campaign meeting. And a speaker and consultant in Roosevelt's entourage was the twenty-nine-year-old Orson Welles, already famous for his panic-creating radio version of H.G. Wells's *War of the Worlds* and for his films such as *The Magnificent Ambersons* and *Citizen Kane*.

For a man with his increasing physical disadvantages Roosevelt fought a vigorous and successful campaign. And on 7 November, 1944 the voters of America elected him to an unprecedented fourth term in the White House. Even though his percentage of the popular vote was, at 52.8%, the lowest of his four presidential elections, Roosevelt was jubilant. And from across the Atlantic, Churchill, now able to be very much on the record congratulated the President with a set of rhetorical flourishes. 'I always said that a great people could be trusted to stand by the pilot who weathered the storm. It is an indescribable relief to me that our comradeship will continue and will help to bring the world out of misery.'

But even at this moment of relief and celebration, Churchill could not forget one of the niggles that he had long had against the President. This was his recollection that Roosevelt had not responded to his congratulatory message at the time of the last presidential election, exactly four years before. But now the President insisted that he had received, and read and certainly not disregarded Churchill's congratulations on that previous victory. He wrote, 'Thank you for your friendly message and for your repetition of the 1940 message which I had not forgotten.' The tending of a large but fragile ego of the other elderly male genius was a task to which each of them always felt it necessary to devote himself. (A similar solicitude shows itself in the friendship between the statesman Georges Clemenceau and the painter Claude Monet.)

A few weeks after his election Roosevelt made his careful gesture of congratulation on Churchill's approaching seventieth birthday. He sent him a printed quotation from Abraham Lincoln accompanied by his own joking comment, 'For Winston on his Birthday – I would go even to Teheran to be with him again.' Obviously Roosevelt remembered the drawbacks of that particular, distant meeting place but he also remembered the good times. On Churchill's actual birthday he cabled, 'Ever so many happy returns of the day. I shall never forget the party with you and UJ [Uncle Joe] a year ago and we must have more of them that are even better.'

The urgent need for another meeting with Stalin was something Roosevelt and Churchill corresponded about a great deal at this time. But arranging it proved difficult because Stalin again insisted that he would not leave the Soviet Union and that the western leaders should come to him. At the same time that different venues were being proposed, political disagreements between Churchill and Roosevelt began to intensify. It would seem that the prospect of victory allowed divergences to express themselves; whilst victory had still to be assured they had been suppressed. Certainly in the last two months of 1944 the differences between the two men were more numerous and more acute than ever before. These weeks marked the lowest point in the many ups and downs their friendship had experienced over the years.

One important cause of division was France. When in November Churchill went to Paris to observe the new French government and to confer with de Gaulle, Roosevelt sent good wishes, 'My best to you on your Paris trip,' but also continued, 'Don't turn up in French clothes'. In one way this was Roosevelt joshing Churchill about the pleasure he took in all kinds of dressing up. But in another way it was a warning about becoming too much of a French sympathiser. And Churchill's stay in Paris did move him in this direction. 'What a change in fortunes since Casablanca,' he remarked in his report to the President. 'Generally I felt in the presence of an organised government, broadly based and of rapidly growing strength.' Churchill was so impressed by de Gaulle's government that he was sympathetic to de Gaulle's desire to attend the next Allied summit with Stalin. But Roosevelt, still strongly hostile to de Gaulle and unimpressed by France and its prospects, would have none of this. Brusquely he replied to Churchill, 'It does not seem to me that the French Provisional Government should take part in our next conference as such a debating society would confuse our essential issues.' Roosevelt prevailed but Churchill still sought to promote France as a major power and a major force in Europe. Such intentions created a continuing friction with the President. William Hazlitt once said that discussing the weakness of acquaintances was 'a great sweetener and cement of friendship'. But the days when Churchill and Roosevelt could sympathise at length about 'the impossible de Gaulle' were over.

A month after Churchill had visited Paris there opened in Chicago a Civil Aviation Conference at which Britain and America sought to agree on the allocation of international air-routes in the post-war world. The Americans wanted them all to be open to free competition. The British knowing the Americans would be so much stronger financially and commercially sought to maintain a degree of imperial preference and monopoly in the air transport industry. It was yet one more instance of an older imperialism seeking to defend itself against a new one. There were acrimonious arguments in Chicago. And the negotiations there rapidly involved the President and the Prime Minister in their confrontations. The exchanges between the two leaders became uncomfortably blunt.

Also in that December the developing crisis in newly liberated Greece had an effect on their relationship. The Prime Minister who insisted and ensured that Greece was a British sphere of influence, wished to preserve the Greek monarchy and to contain the influence of the socialists and communists. British troops in Greece soon found themselves fighting against the forces of the left. Elliott Roosevelt remembered his father's disgust at the situation.

> 'I wouldn't be surprised,' he went on, 'if Winston had simply made it clear he was backing the Greek Royalists. That would only be in character. But killing Greek guerillas! Using British soldiers for such a job!'
> 'Probably using American Lend Lease equipment to do it too,' I reminded him.
> 'I'll find out about *that*,' Father said.[3]

Churchill's deep belief in the monarchical principle also showed itself in his dealings with the post-occupation regimes in Belgium and Italy. In the case of Italy tension between Churchill and the Americans intensified danger-ously. The inclusion of Count Sforza, a long-time opponent to Mussolini, in a new Italian government came to be the crux of the issue. And there came a point when Roosevelt's new Secretary of State, Edward R. Stettinius, dispensed with diplomatic niceties and openly criticised British opposition to Sforza. Churchill was incensed, in great part because he felt that the President was a party to the rebuke. He told Roosevelt, 'I was much hurt that a difference about Count Sforza should have been made the occasion for an attempt on the part of the State Department to administer a public rebuke to His Majesty's Government'.[4] And to Harry Hopkins, now in slightly better health, and returned to a position of favour and influence in the White House Churchill complained resentfully, 'I consider we have a right to the President's support in the policy we are following ... It grieves me very much to see signs of our drifting apart at a time when unity becomes even more important, as danger recedes and faction arises.'[5] As so often in the old days Churchill was using Harry Hopkins as a way of speaking to the President without actually speaking to the President.

It was fortunate that Christmas was fast approaching. Hurt and angry reproaches could be replaced by warm seasonal greetings. And with the coming of the New Year President and Prime Minister became increasingly concerned with arranging their meeting with Stalin in Russia to which, Roosevelt had finally conceded, they would set off at the end of January 1945. Their destination was the Crimean resort town of Yalta on the Black Sea. Churchill, always mindful of classical history and myth suggested to Roosevelt that this coming conference be codenamed ARGONAUT. For when Jason and his crew of heroes, the Argonauts, had set off on their quest for the Golden Fleece they had headed for Colchis, an ancient kingdom on the eastern shore of the Black Sea. Roosevelt readily accepted the suggestion, remarking that he and Churchill also were beginning an heroic quest. 'Your suggestion of ARGONAUT is welcomed. You and I are direct descendants.'

Roosevelt and Churchill may well have hoped for some glittering prizes from their long journey to Yalta but they had also, first of all, to lose face. For once again Stalin had his way as to the venue. He claimed his doctors refused to condone his leaving the Soviet Union and so Roosevelt, by now a dying man, and Churchill, whose health was precarious, had to make the long journey to the Crimea. The unmistakable political implication of this was that Russia was the dominant power in the anti-Nazi alliance. Roosevelt and Churchill had more to ask of Stalin than he of them. The Soviet Union was at the summit of its military, political and diplomatic power. Roosevelt and Churchill needed Stalin's assistance in the same way that some three years before at Placentia Bay in Newfoundland Churchill had needed Roosevelt's.

Roosevelt was inaugurated President for the fourth time on 20 January, 1945. Just forty-eight hours later he secretly left the White House and began the long, arduous journey to meet with Stalin in the Soviet Union. He travelled first to Newport in Virginia where as a man of naval interests and background he took immense pleasure in being the Commander in Chief and thus the one to give the order for the heavy cruiser USS *Quincy* and its accompanying vessels to get under way. With his daughter, Mrs Anna Boettiger to attend him the President enjoyed the voyage and especially his sixty-third birthday party which was held in his quarters.

It took the *Quincy* some ten days to reach the British ruled island of Malta in the Mediterranean. As the large, grey American warship entered the sunny, shimmering harbour, the President, looking very frail and wearing an unfamiliar tweed cap was wheeled up on deck. And there awaiting him was the British ship HMS *Orion* with Churchill, Eden, the British Chiefs of Staff and their American counterparts who had arrived earlier, all standing on deck and waving in welcome. The British were saddened by the further deterioration in the President's appearance. Gentle Marian Holmes, one of Churchill's secretaries, wrote, 'What a change in the President since we saw him in Hyde Park last October. He seems to have lost so much weight, has dark circles under his eyes, looks altogether frail and as if he is hardly in this world at all.'[6] Churchill accompanied by his daughter Sarah and by his Foreign Secretary, Anthony Eden, quickly transferred to the American ship. The two leaders greeted each other warmly and Churchill and his party stayed to lunch. Admiral Leahy, the President's new adviser, and far more conservative than Harry Hopkins, dined with them. Over the meal Roosevelt was subdued but made it plain that he was unwilling to discuss issues of political importance. Churchill, Admiral Leahy remembered, was extremely talkative, lecturing the table on England's wartime problems, the high purposes of the so-called Atlantic Charter and 'his complete devotion to the principles enunciated in America's Declaration of Independence'. Roosevelt had heard such self recommendation often enough before. But he was keen to get past the painful disagreements of the weeks before Christmas. So he listened courteously and also made the kind of gesture that always touched Churchill. The President had a candle placed on the dining table near to Churchill so that his guest might light his cigar.

The following day began the task of moving the two delegations on to the next stage of their long journey. Some seven hundred and fifty persons had to be flown from Malta, across the Mediterranean, Greece, the Aegean and the Black Sea to Saki airfield in the Crimea. To deal with all the delegates, their luggage and equipment transport planes took off from Malta at ten-minute intervals from half past eleven at night until dawn. Roosevelt, flying in Sacred Cow was badly shaken up by the flight. His plane had to fly uncomfortably high over the mountains of Greece. One of his six escorting fighter planes could not make it and had to turn back. Thick ice formed on the wings of Sacred Cow. The Secret Service men debated in an urgent whisper the advantages and disadvantages of putting the Mae West lifebelt on the President.

After finally arriving at the remote military airbase at Saki, the President and Prime Minister and their parties faced a ninety mile drive over dangerous mountain roads to the coastal resort of Yalta. The sparsely populated landscape showed the signs of the heavy fighting that had taken place between the Russians and Germans in the Crimea less than a year before. There were many gutted, blackened buildings, derailed German freight trains and charred tanks, their guns pointing up at crazy angles. The Russian chauffeurs drove fast along the steep, winding mountain roads. At brief regular intervals by the roadside stood members of the Red Army, many of them young women, saluting the visitors. The President, travelling in a car with his daughter Anna, was intrigued and stimulated by this wild ride. He had always been interested in geography and in remote, unfamiliar places and the snowy winter landscape of the Crimea exhilarated him. When he finally arrived at Yalta he was met by Averell Harriman's daughter Kathleen who was serving as hostess for her father who was now American Ambassador to the Soviet Union. Greeting the President on this occasion Kathleen found him neither unwell nor travel weary. Rather, she wrote, 'He's absolutely charming, easy to talk to, with a lovely sense of humour'.[7]

After the Yalta Conference was over *Time* magazine reminded its readers that this was not the first time the little Crimean resort had captured the interest of a distinguished American. Nearly eighty years before, just after the American Civil War ended, Mark Twain had visited Yalta and given an admiring description of it in his book *Innocents Abroad*. (*Time* seems to imply that the title has a relevance to Roosevelt's expedition to meet and deal with Stalin.) Yalta and its surroundings reminded Twain of the sierras he had known as a young journalist in what was then Nevada Territory. He wrote:

> To me the place was a vision of the Sierras. The tall gray mountains that back it, their sides bristling with pines – cloven with ravines – here and there a heavy rock towering into view – long straight streaks sweeping down from the summit to the sea, marking the passage of some avalanche of former times – all these were as like one sees in the Sierras as if the one were a portrait of the other. The little village of Yalta nestles at the foot of an ampitheatre which slopes backward and upward to the wall of hills, and looks as if it might have sunk quietly down to its present position from a high elevation. This depression is covered with great parks and gardens of noblemen, and through the mass of green foliage the bright colours of their palaces look out here and there like flowers. It is a beautiful spot.

The great holiday villa to which Roosevelt was taken was the Livadia Palace. It was built of white Crimean granite and stood high on a bluff, a hundred and fifty feet above the Black Sea. It commanded spectacular views of the ocean and of the snow-capped mountains to landward. Its extensive gardens were filled with cypress, cedar and yew trees. The fifty room palace had been built for Czar Nicholas in 1911 and he and the Russian royal family had spent many summers there. Roosevelt occupied the Czar's suite and the rest of his party had lesser quarters. There was much ribald humour among the Americans when it was learned that Admiral King, the tough guy, was occupying the Czarina's boudoir which was approached by a concealed external stone staircase, often used, so the rumour ran, by Rasputin. In his memoirs the Admiral, writing of himself, as always, in the third person, and rather stiffly, conceded that 'King had her boudoir which led to some jesting ...' But then he proceeded to what were for him more serious problems with the accommodation at Yalta '... there were never enough towels to go round, and as there was only one bathroom to a floor, considerable time was spent getting in to it.'[8] Other western participants at the conference became preoccupied with this latter problem. 'Excepting only the war,' said one, 'the bathrooms were the most generally discussed subject at the Crimean Conference.'

For all its outside regal grandeur the Livadia Palace was on the inside, in 1945, a shabby, poorly furnished place. The retreating Germans had stripped it of all its fittings and, for the conference, the Soviets had had to transport ill-assorted chairs, tables, couches, crockery, cutlery and office furniture from all over their ravaged country. The contrast between this new Russia and the old, the many reminders of the fate of the Romanovs and then of Hitler's army and the suggestion that Rasputin's ghost might visit and seek to charm Admiral King in his royal boudoir, all contributed to the sense of the surreal and the crazy which was shared by several of those taking part in the historic conference.

The conference lasted some eight days and in the plenary sessions led by the three governmental leaders and in subsidiary gatherings issues as diverse as the constitution of the proposed Security Council of the

United Nations, the amount of German reparation, the difficult problem of Poland, its borders and future government, the entry of the Soviet Union into the Pacific War and the administration of a defeated Germany were all taken up. But Poland was the issue to which by far the greatest amount of time was devoted. To many the phrase 'the Yalta Conference' still has pejorative connotations. The Western Allies, it has been argued, were, at best, deluded by Stalin and the Soviet delegates. Or, at the worst, the West sold out, tacitly consigning the nations of Eastern Europe to more than two generations of harsh, Soviet domination. Whatever the truth of it, there can be no doubt that important agreements entered into at Yalta did not last. Very shortly after the conference had ended, Churchill, always more sceptical about Stalin than Roosevelt was at this time, became distressed and angry at the way the Soviet Union reneged on its commitment to free and open elections in Poland. He would feel intensely the painful irony that Britain, which had entered the war to honour a commitment to assist Poland against Hitler, was now forced to stand by impotently and watch Poland taken over by Stalin.

But, one wonders, could more have been achieved by the West at Yalta? Certain inevitabilities were making themselves obvious. There was the sheer mass of Red Army power in eastern Europe. There was America's urgent need for Soviet help in defeating the Japanese. And there was, plain for all to see, the dying of the President of the United States. The conference may have ended in a mood of euphoric optimism, there may have been the same ten-course meals and the multiple toasts as on previous occasions and the same flattering speeches (speeches which someone like Brooke now saw degenerating into 'insincere, slimy sort of slush') but major disagreements between east and west were disguised rather than resolved. Stalin at the height of his political skills which were much admired by western observers was clearly aware of the military and economic limitations of Britain and of the increasing leaderlessness of the United States. At many of the plenary sessions in the great banqueting hall of the Palace, the President in his wheelchair at the head of the table was dreamily silent. On other occasions, perhaps sensing how little time there was left to him, he would want complex matters settled in haste. And at other times he would make speeches that wandered off into extended irrelevance, as when, for instance, in the second plenary session the future of Germany was being discussed and the President entered into a long, rambling discourse about the bucolic, cultured, pre-militarist Germany he had known as a schoolboy on his first visit to Europe almost sixty years before. As one of Roosevelt's biographers has observed, the goings on at Yalta had something of the absurdism of Lewis Carroll's *Alice in Wonderland*.[9] The three elderly leaders talked and drank and ate and toasted each other. But the actualities of the world war played themselves out athwart the decisions worked out and enunciated in this shabby palace by the sea.

And then, abruptly and disconcertingly, Roosevelt announced that he was leaving the conference. Churchill, aware of how much still needed to be thrashed out with Stalin, protested violently, 'Franklin, you cannot go!' But the President would not hear him. The friendship was attentuating due to Roosevelt's illness and weariness. There was kindness but there was also ever-increasing distance between them. It was as though they could no longer hear each other. Sad to say, on the voyage back to America what would prove to be Roosevelt's final goodbye to Harry Hopkins would be said in petulance and anger. There was no such break with Churchill.

Rather, due to Roosevelt's health, there was a petering out of that acute political and human sense of each other which they had previously had. At the last, at Yalta Churchill became irritated and frustrated by Roosevelt's dreamy indifference to the proceedings of the conference. 'The President is behaving very badly,' he complained to a member of his entourage. 'He won't take any interest in what we are trying to do.'[10]

There was to be one final meeting between the two men, a calm, gentle coda to their long, eventful and creative friendship. For after the two of them had left Yalta separately, they came together one last time, en route home, off the coast of Egypt.

Churchill flew from Russia to Greece. After a speech to a vast crowd in Constitution Square in Athens, a speech which helped confirm the Greek regency and the political compromise he had helped build on his visit at Christmas, Churchill flew on to the port of Alexandria. Here launches bore him and his party out into the shimmering blue waters of the Mediterranean. A mile or so offshore the USS *Quincy* rode at anchor with the President on board resting after a harrowing journey back from the Crimea. With an effort the President got himself ready to host his visitors at a lunch party. Those there remembered it as a quiet, pleasant, kindly occasion. There was talk between the two men of family members and hobbies and the black thirties Packard in which Stalin and Molotov had driven to the sessions at Yalta. They talked of the final surreal image that the Crimea had presented to them in the drive to the airport, the colossal heap of Russian locomotives – a thousand or more – which had been pitched into a chasm by the Germans before they quitted – the wheels and pistons and smoke stacks all pointing in different directions. Then they talked of Clementine's coming goodwill trip to Russia and then of some shared memories. Churchill was not hectoring as he had been at the previous lunch on the *Quincy*. He was tactfully subdued and very charming. 'It was a pleasant social occasion in the President's cabin,' recalled Admiral Leahy, 'and I do not recall that affairs of state entered into the conversation.'[11]

When the lunch ended and Roosevelt showed signs of weariness Churchill rose to say goodbye. He held the President's emaciated hand in both of his and spoke to him affectionately in a low voice for an extended period of time. Then, his eyes moist, he turned away, quickly left the cabin and returned to his launch tied up alongside the *Quincy*. The two men would never meet again. Some years later Churchill remembered the President's 'placid, frail aspect' on that last day. And the Prime Minister's subsequent comments years later, in his memoirs, were brief and simple, those of someone seeking to stay away from emotional complexities and depths. 'This was the last time I saw Roosevelt. We parted affectionately. I felt he had a slender contact with life.'

In the fifty-seven days the President had left to him after that last meeting on 15 February 1945, his side of the resumed correspondence with Churchill was for the most part composed by Admiral Leahy and by government officials, chiefly from the State Department. In March, Judge Samuel Rosenman, a close political friend and adviser to the President, arrived in Britain to discuss with Churchill Britain's problems with food supplies. Rosenman was also able to give the Prime Minister a vivid sense of the President's now unquestionably terminal condition. So Churchill, though very much at odds with the American administration on how to deal with Stalin's abrogation of the agreements made at Yalta concerning

Poland, employed the utmost tact and consideration in his communications with the President. One of his last personal messages, sent in the middle of March, is full of reassurance, referring confidently to 'your long promised visit to Britain'. It is also a statement of personal feeling and gratitude. It reads like a summing up of what their friendship has been and what it has achieved as a force in planetary history or in what Churchill calls the 'World Cause'. Churchill's telegram said, 'I hope that the rather numerous telegrams I have to send you on so many of our difficult and intertwined affairs are not becoming a bore to you. Our friendship is the rock on which I build for the future of the world so long as I am one of the builders. I always think of those tremendous days when you devised Lend-Lease, when we met at Argentia, when you decided with my heartfelt agreement to launch the invasion of Africa, and when you comforted me for the loss of Tobruk by giving me the 300 Shermans of subsequent Alamein fame. I remember the part our personal relations have played in the advance of the World Cause ...'[12]

Three and a half weeks after sending this message, Churchill working late as usual in the Downing Street Annexe was informed by one of his aides that the President had died at his home in Warm Springs, Georgia. The Prime Minister, though half expecting such news, was overwhelmed. He paced about, no longer able to work or concentrate. To his wife who was on a goodwill tour of the Soviet Union he sent a telegram telling her of 'the grievous news'. He paced and drank brandy. He went to bed but could not sleep. He reported to one of his aides, 'I am much weakened in every way by his loss'. Very early the following morning he wrote telegrams of condolence. The one to Eleanor Roosevelt was formal and rhetorical. The one to Harry Hopkins expressed more personal feeling and alluded to the complex two-faceted relationship, the personal and the political which he had known with Roosevelt. That telegram read, 'I feel with you that we have lost one of our greatest friends and one of the most valiant champions of the causes for which we fight. I feel a very painful personal loss quite apart from the ties of public action which bound us so closely together. I had a true affection for Franklin.'[13]

And then later that day Churchill went to the House of Commons where he moved the adjournment of the House as a mark of respect to the President's memory. Those who listened to him were impressed by how upset the Prime Minister was. Harold Nicolson, a far less cynical diarist of that time than 'Chips' Channon wrote of that parliamentary occasion. 'I feel deeply for Winston … this afternoon it was evident from his manner that it was a real body-blow.' Four days later in St Paul's Cathedral there was held the great memorial service for the President after which Churchill wept openly and long. Later the Prime Minister returned to the House of Commons to make his final, considered, parliamentary statement about his relationship with the President. It had been, at its simplest, he had worked out, a matter of nine wartime meetings and 'over 1,700 messages'. But from these there had developed close and complex ties on both the personal and the political level. Of his personal bond with Roosevelt Churchill spoke only briefly and retiringly. 'I felt the utmost confidence in his upright, inspiring character and outlook, and a personal regard – affection I must say – for him beyond my power to express today.' Churchill then went on to give his assessment of the political Roosevelt in two sentences that are full of feeling yet carefully worded and devoid of rhetoric. At the centre of both sentences is the metaphor of 'heart' which Churchill, like many others, saw as indicating one of the chief qualities of the thirty-second president. To his fellow parliamentarians Churchill

Coda

concluded of Roosevelt the politician:

> His love of his country, his respect for its constitution, his power of gauging the tides and currents of its mobile public opinion, were always evident, but added to these were the beatings of that generous heart which was always stirred to anger and to action by spectacles of aggression and oppression by the strong against the weak. It is, indeed, a loss, a bitter loss to humanity that those heart-beats are stilled for ever.

Notes

1. Kimball, p. 337.
2. Ibid., p. 341.
3. Elliott Roosevelt, p. 223.
4. Kimball, p. 438.
5. Gilbert, p. 1096.
6. Ibid., p. 1167.
7. Harriman, p. 391.
8. King and Muirhead, p. 589.
9. Ted Morgan, *F.D.R.* (New York, 1983), p. 748.
10. Moran, p. 198.
11. Ernest J. Leahy, *I Was There* (New York, Harpers, 1953), p. 327.
12. Gilbert, p. 1254.
13. Ibid., p. 1291.

Select Bibliography

Adams, Henry H., *Harry Hopkins, A Biography* (New York, 1977)

Alexander of Tunis, Earl, *Memoirs* (Cassell, 1962)

Alldritt, Keith, *Churchill the Writer: His Life as a Man of Letters* (Hutchinson, 1992)

Argyle, Christopher, *Chronology of World War II* (Marshall Cavendish, 1980)

Beschloss, Michael, *Kennedy and Roosevelt, The Uneasy Alliance* (W.W. Norton, New York, 1980)

Bishop, Jim, *FDR's Last Year: April 1944–April 1945* (Pocket Books, New York, 1975)

Bryant, Arthur, *The Turn of The Tide* (Doubleday, New York, 1957)

Bryant, Arthur, *Triumph In The West* (Doubleday, Garden City, 1959)

Burns, James MacGregor, *Roosevelt: The Lion and the Fox* (Harcourt Brace Jovanovich, New York, 1956)

Burns, James MacGregor, *Roosevelt: Soldier of Freedom, 1940–45* (Harcourt Brace Jovanovich, New York, 1970)

Carter, Violet Bonham, *Winston Churchill As I Knew Him* (Eyre & Spottiswoode, 1965)

Churchill, Sarah, *A Thread in the Tapestry* (Andre Deutsch, 1967)

Churchill, Sarah, *Keep On Dancing* (Weidenfeld and Nicolson, 1981)

Churchill, Winston S., *The Second World War*, 6 vols (Cassell, 1948–53)

Clemens, Diane Shaver, *Yalta* (Oxford University Press, New York, 1970)

Colville, John, *The Fringes of Power: Downing Street Diaries 1939–1955* (Hodder & Stoughton, 1985)

Conant, James B., *My Several Lives* (Harper, New York, 1970)

Dallek, Robert, *Franklin D. Roosevelt and American Foreign Policy, 1932–1945* (Oxford University Press, New York, 1979)

Dilks, David (ed.) *The Diaries of Sir Alexander Cadogan O.M. 1938–1945* (Cassell, 1971)

Divine, R., *Roosevelt and World War II*, (Johns Hopkins, Baltimore Md, 1969)

Dows, Olin, *Franklin Roosevelt at Hyde Park* (American Artists Group, New York, 1949)

Eden Anthony, *The Memoirs: The Reckoning* (Cassell, 1965)

Eisenhower, D.D., *Crusade in Europe* (Doubleday, New York, 1948)

Eubank, Keith, *Summit At Teheran: The Untold Story* (William Morrow, New York, 1985)

Eubank, Keith, *The Summit Conferences, 1919–1960* (Norman, Oklahoma, 1966)

Feis, Herbert, *Churchill, Roosevelt, Stalin: The War They Waged and the Peace They Sought*, (Princeton University Press, Princeton, 1957)

Francisco, Charles, *You Must Remember This: The Filming of Casablanca* (Prentice-Hall, New Jersey, 1980)

Fraser, Sir D., *Alanbrooke* (Collins, 1982)

Gilbert, Martin, *Winston S. Churchill: 1941–1945* (Heinemann, 1986)

Harriman, W. Averell & Abel Elie, *Special Envoy to Churchill and Stalin 1941–46* (Random House, New York, 1975)

Harvey, John (ed.), *The War Diaries of Oliver Harvey 1941–1945* (Collins, 1978)

Hassett, William D., *Off the Record with F.D.R. 1942–1945* (Rutgers University Press, New Brunswick, 1958)

Ismay, General Lord, *The Memoirs of General Lord Ismay* (Viking Press, New York, 1960)

Kennan, George F., *Memoirs 1925–50* (*Atlantic Monthly*, Little, Brown, Boston, 1955)

King, Ernest J., and Whitehill, Walter Muir, *Fleet Admiral King: A Naval Record* (Harper, New York, 1953)

Kimball, Warren F. (ed.) *Churchill & Roosevelt: The Complete Correspondence*, 3 Vols. (Princeton University Press, Princeton 1984)

Kimball, Warren F., *The Juggler: Franklin Roosevelt as Wartime Statesman* (Princeton University Press, Princeton, 1991)

Lash, Joseph P. (ed.) *From The Diaries of Felix Frankfurter* (Norton, New York, 1975)

Lash, Joseph P., *Roosevelt and Churchill* (Andre Deutsch, 1977)

Leahy, William D., *I Was There* (McGraw Hill, New York, 1950)

Loewenheim, Francis L., Langley, Harold D. & Jonas, Manfred (eds) *Roosevelt and Churchill: Their Secret Wartime Correspondence* (Barrie & Jenkins, 1975)

Louis, Wm. Roger, *Imperialism at Bay: The United States and the Decolonization of the British Empire, 1941–1945* (Oxford University Press, New York, 1978)

McIntire, Vice Admiral Ross T., *White House Physician* (Putnams, New York, 1946)

Macmillan, Harold, *The Blast of War, 1939–1945* (Harper and Row, New York, 1968)

Mcneil, W.H., *America, Britain and Russia: Their Cooperation and Conflict, 1941–1946* (Oxford University Press, 1953)

Mannin, Ethel, *Moroccan Mosaic* (Jarrolds, 1953)

Moran, Lord, *Winston Churchill: The Struggle for Survival 1940–1965* (Constable, 1966)

Morton, H.V., *Atlantic Meeting* (Methuen & Co. Ltd, 1943)

Select Bibliography

Nicolson, Nigel (ed.) *The War Years, 1939–1945. Vol II of The Diaries and Letters of Harold Nicolson* (Atheneum, New York, 1967)

O'Connor, Raymond G., *Diplomacy for Victory: FDR and Unconditional Surrender* (W.W. Norton, New York, 1971)

Orwell, George, *Collected Essays* (Secker and Warburg, 1961)

Pawle, Gerald, *The War and Colonel Warden* (George Harrap and Co., 1963)

Perkins, Frances, *The Roosevelt I Knew* (Harper, New York, 1946)

Pogue, Forrest C., *George C. Marshall: Ordeal and Hope, 1939–1942* (Viking, New York, 1966)

Pogue, Forrest C., *George C. Marshall: Organizer of Victory, 1943–1945* (Viking, New York, 1973)

Rhodes James, Robert, *Churchill: A Study in Failure 1900–1939* (Weidenfeld & Nicolson, 1990)

Rigdon, William M., *White House Sailor* (Doubleday, Garden City, 1962)

Rollins, Alfred B., *Roosevelt and Howe* (Knopf, New York, 1962)

Roosevelt, Eleanor, *This I Remember* (Harper, New York, 1949)

Roosevelt, Elliott, *As He Saw It* (Duell, Sloan and Pearce, New York, 1946)

Roosevelt, Elliott (ed.) *The Roosevelt Letters*, 3 Vols. (George G. Harrap & Co. Ltd., 1952)

Roosevelt, Elliott and Brough, James, *A Rendezvous with Destiny: The Roosevelts of the White House* (W.H. Allen, 1972)

Roosevelt, Elliott and Brough, James, *An Untold Story: The Roosevelts of Hyde Park* (W.H. Allen, 1974)

Rosenman, Samuel I., *Working with Roosevelt* (Da Capo, New York, 1972)

Sainsbury, Keith, *The Turning Point* (Oxford University Press, Oxford, 1986)

Sherwood, Robert E., *Roosevelt and Hopkins: An Intimate History* (Harper and Brothers, New York, 1948)

Soames, Mary, *Clementine Churchill* (Cassell, 1979)

Spring, Howard, *In The Meantime* (Constable, 1942)

Stettinius, Edward R., Jr., *Roosevelt and the Russians: The Yalta Conference* (Doubleday, Garden City, 1949)

Stevenson, William, *A Man Called Intrepid* (Macmillan, 1976)

Terraine, J., *The Life and Times of Lord Mountbatten* (Hutchinson, 1968)

Tuchman, Barbara, *Stilwell and the American Experience in China, 1911– 1945* (Macmillan, 1971)

Tugwell, Rexford G., *F.D.R. Architect of an Era* (Macmillan, New York, 1967)

Wilson, Theodore A., *The First Summit: Roosevelt and Churchill at Placentia Bay 1941* (Houghton Mifflin, Boston, 1969)

Index

Abel, Elie, 122
Achilles, HMS, 37
Ajax, HMS, 37
Alexander, General Sir Harold, 112, 194
Alice in Wonderland, 210
American Civil War, 131, 134
Argentia Bay, 58, 77, 213
Argonaut, 203
Arkansas, USS, 58
Asquith, Violet, 133
Atlantic Charter, 66, 68, 70
Atlas Mountains, 118–22, 163, 184
Augusta, USS, 57, 58, 59, 61, 62, 64, 67, 68, 72, 88
Austen, Jane, 182

Babes on Broadway, 51
Badoglio, General Pietro, 143
Baltimore, USS, 188
Baruch, Bernard, 23–4, 185
Basic English, 186–7
Bathurst, 123
Battle of Britain, 40
Battle of the River Plate, 38–9
Beaverbrook, Lord, 52, 71, 128, 184
Benes, President Eduard, 184
Bergman, Ingrid, 107, 109
Bethesda Naval Hospital, 153
Bevan, Aneurin, 100
Bismarck, 46, 54, 57
Blitz, The, 40, 60, 72
Boer War, 28, 79
Boettiger, Anna, 204
Bogart, Humphrey, 107, 109
Boswell, James, 85
Bracken, Brendan, 52, 53, 63
Braun, Eva, 20

British Guyana, 41
Brooke, General Alan, 83, 90, 113, 117, 146, 160, 161, 164, 169, 175, 178, 181, 186, 209
Bryant, Arthur, 97, 122, 166, 179
Bucaneer, 177, 178
Burns, Robert, 99
Byron, Lord, 82

Cadogan, Sir Alexander, 54, 56, 58, 65, 66, 67, 86, 149, 161, 186, 193, 196
Cairo, 157, 158, 160, 177, 192
Camp David, 106
Carroll, Lewis, 210
Carthage, 139
Casablanca, 107
Casablanca, 104, 107, 108, 109, 111, 113, 115, 117, 125, 183, 210
Chamberlain, Neville, 33, 39
Channon, Sir Henry 'Chips', 25–6, 35, 214
Chaplin, Charles, 24
Chatta Nooga Choo Choo, 117
Chesterfield, Lord, 181
Chiang-Kai-shek, Generalissimo, 157, 158, 160, 161, 165, 177
Chiang-Kai-shek, Madame, 161, 162, 165
Chicago Tribune, 153
Churchill, Clementine, 25, 87, 101, 105, 124, 144, 145, 151, 182, 190, 211
Churchill, Lord Randolph, 27
Churchill, Mary, 101, 144, 145, 149, 151, 182, 190, 211
Churchill, Randolph, 61, 72, 175, 182
Churchill, Sarah, 160, 162, 164, 166,

Index

175, 179
Churchill, Winston S.
  birthday party of, 173–5
  and ceremonial, 62, 175
  and the classics, 14, 116, 139, 158, 203
  and concern for FDR, 140–1
  and conferences: Cairo, 159–65; Casablanca, 109–18; Placentia Bay, 58–71; Quebec I, 143–8; Quebec II, 192–4; Teheran, 168–77; Washington I, 77–83; Washington II, 93–6; Washington III, 129–37; Yalta, 206–11
  and death of FDR, 23–6, 213–15
  and dress, 53, 90, 121, 167, 170, 201
  and Eleanor Roosevelt, 105, 131, 146
  family background, 15
  and films, 24, 57, 72, 125, 149, 191, 197
  first meeting with FDR, 26–30
  and food, 56, 80, 102–3, 163, 191
  and Hopkins, 43–4, 55, 100, 113, 203
  and literature, 82, 124, 128, 131–3, 168, 182, 186–7
  as orator, 65–6, 135–6, 187, 211, 214–15
  and the press, 77–8, 114–15
  and New Deal, 32–3
  and serious illness, 181–4
  as writer, 35, 37, 82, 88
Citizen Kane, 199
Clark, General Mark, 116
Clemenceau, Georges, 200
Clinton, William, 61
Clough, Arthur Hugh, 46
Cockran, Bourke, 27
Colville, John, 196
Compiègne, 39
Conant, Dr James B., 149
Constantine, 129
Crete, 47

Dardanelles, 29
Deep in the Heart of Texas, 117
Defoe, Daniel, 124

de Gaulle, General Charles, 112–14, 125, 126, 136, 141, 147, 168, 184, 210
Delano, Laura, 21
Desert Victory, 125
Dewey, Thomas E., 197, 198
Dickens, Charles, 168
Dill, Sir John, 53
Diocletian, 129
Dragoon, 189
Duke of York, HMS, 76, 77, 83
Dunkirk, 39, 82, 155

Eden, Anthony, 85, 116, 161, 165, 166, 167, 171, 205
Eisenhower, General Dwight D., 112, 113, 114, 126, 134, 137, 139, 159, 181, 184
Exeter, HMS, 37

Fala, 65, 198
Fall of France, 40, 45
Final Solution, 51
Fitzgerald, Scott, 61
Frankland, Air Commodore, see Churchill, Winston
Franklin D. Roosevelt Jones, 48, 50, 51
Frederick, Md., 131, 135
Freeman, Sir Wilfred, 53
Frietchie, Barbara, 131, 135

Garland, Judy, 51, 149
George VI, King, 62, 70, 99, 143, 172
Georgia Warm Springs Foundation, 18
Gettysburg, Pa., 133, 135
Gilbert and Sullivan, 183
Gilbert Martin, S., 84, 97, 122, 137, 152, 196, 215
Giraud, General Henri, 112, 113, 125
Gloucester, Duke of, 99
Gneisenau, 85
Goering, Hermann, 26, 51
Gordon, General Charles George, 82
Graf Spee, 38
Gray's Inn, London, 29
Grinnell, Ia., 32
Groton, 18

Index

Hackensack, 92
Hardy, Oliver, 72
Harriman, Averell, 60, 61, 65, 71, 86, 96, 102, 114, 115, 122, 128, 141, 147–8, 152, 169, 171, 175, 179, 215
Harriman, Kathleen, 206
Harriman, Pamela, 61
Harvard, 18, 149
Hazlitt, William, 201
Heights of Abraham, The, 144
Heydrich, Reinhard, 51
Hitler, Adolf, 15, 20, 26, 33, 40, 42, 47, 51, 77, 143, 155, 209
Holmes, Marian, 195, 205
Hope, Bob, 149
Hopkins Harry, 31, 33–4, 40, 43, 44, 48, 55–7, 61, 65, 69, 71, 77, 88, 93, 96, 97, 100, 106, 108, 111, 113, 115, 118, 126, 128, 131, 135–6, 148, 151, 153–5, 159, 164, 182, 185, 203, 205, 210, 213
Hopkins, Robert, 159, 164
Howe, Louis B., 31, 34
Hull, Cordell, 61
Hyde Park, 15, 17, 18, 91–2, 123, 145–6, 148–51, 163, 183, 194, 205

Ignatiev, Count Alexander Pavlovich, 153
India, 28
Iowa, USS, 158, 159, 178
Ismay, Hastings (Pug), 83, 90, 94, 95, 97, 137, 152, 175, 178, 179, 192, 196
Iwo Jima, 17

Jackson, General Stonewall, 131–3
Jason and the Golden Fleece, 203
Jefferson, Thomas, 129
Jerome, Jennie, 27
Johnson, Dr Samuel, 17, 76, 81

Keats, John, 133
Kennedy, Joseph, 43
Kimball, Warren F., 35, 48, 49, 84, 97, 122, 137, 152, 166, 196, 215
King, Admiral Ernest J., 164, 171, 179, 188, 196, 208, 215

King George V, HMS, 184
Kinna, Patrick, 80
Kuomintang, 157

La Rochefoucauld, 37, 167
Lash, Joseph, 42, 49
Laurel, Stan, 72
Leahy, Admiral, 185, 205, 212, 215
Lease-Lend, 43, 48, 68, 191, 213
Lee, Robert E., 133
Leigh, Vivien, 57
Lewis, John L., 140
Lincoln, Abraham, 109, 131
Lindemann, Professor (Lord Cherwell), 54, 65, 193
Litvinov, Maxim, 82
Lloyd George, David, 24, 27, 29
Longfellow, Henry Wadsworth, 44, 45
Louis XIV, 15
Luftwaffe, 40

Macmillan, Harold, 182
Macy, Louise, 96
Marrakesh, 118–20, 123–4, 183–4
Marlborough, Duke of, 15, 35
Marshall, General George, 88, 94, 113, 137, 146
Mayrant, USS, 111
McDougal, USS, 67
Midway, 89
Miller, Glen, 164
Milne, Sir John Wardlow, 99
Missouri Waltz, 117
Molotov, Vyacheslav, 172, 211
Monet, Claude, 200
Montevideo, Uruguay, 38
Montgomery, General Bernard, 17, 102, 125, 184
Moran, Lord Charles, 79, 81, 89, 101, 120, 122, 145, 168, 170, 179, 182, 192–3, 195, 196, 215
Morgan, Ted, 215
Morgenthau, Henry, 193
Morgenthau Plan, 193
Morton, Desmond, 182
Morton, H.V., 52–5, 63, 67, 73
Mountbatten, Admiral Louis, 146
Mussolini, Benito, 15, 77, 203

222

Index

National Geographic Magazine and Society, 123
New Deal, 31–3, 42
Newfoundland, 41, 88, 196
Niagara Falls, 145
Nicholas, Tsar, 207
Nicolson, Harold, 214
Nimitz, Admiral Chester, 188

Odyssey, 158
Ogden, C.K., 187
Oliver, Vic, 160
Olivier, Laurence, 57
Orion, HMS, 205
Overlord, 148, 155, 156, 158, 169, 171, 177, 189

Patton, General, 17
Pavlov, 174, 175
Pearl Harbor, 44, 75, 82, 188
Perkins, Frances, 176, 179
Placentia Bay, 64, 70, 110, 204
Poland, 33
Potomac, 59, 158
Poughkeepsie, 17, 195
Pound, Sir Dudley, 53
Prettyman, Arthur, 22
Prince of Wales, HMS, 46, 54–8, 62, 66, 67, 70, 71, 72, 76
Prinz Eugen, 85
Proust Marcel, 25
Psalms, 106

Quebec, 143–8, 155, 158, 190, 192, 193
Queen Mary, 127–8, 144–5, 191, 195, 197
Quincy, USS, 204, 211, 212

Rasputin, Gregory, 153–4, 208
Renown, HMS, 151
Ribbentrop, Joachim von, 26
Richards, I.A., 187
Rockefeller, John D., 129
Rogers, Captain Kelly, 91
Rommel, Erwin, 88, 99, 160
Rooney, Mickey, 149
Roosevelt, Eleanor, 19, 20, 42, 49, 59, 73, 104, 105, 118, 131, 134–5, 139, 145, 146, 213

Roosevelt, Elliott, 59–62, 67–9, 73, 106, 110, 115, 116, 122, 144, 159, 164, 172, 179, 202, 215
Roosevelt, Franklin D.
  and ceremonial, 59, 62, 67, 72
  and classics, 14, 116, 158, 203
  concern for WSC, 76, 87, 124
  and Conferences: Cairo, 159–65; Casablanca, 109–18; Placentia Bay, 58–71; Quebec I, 143–8; Quebec II, 192–4; Teheran, 168–77; Washington I, 77–83; Washington II, 93–6; Washington III, 129–37; Yalta, 206–11
  death of, 20–3, 213
  domestic politics of, 40–2, 140–1, 151–5, 188, 198–200
  early career of, 17–19
  family background, 15
  first meeting with WSC, 26–30
  and imperialism, 69, 117–18
  and Lucy Mercer, 19–23, 188
  and New Deal 31–3
  personal diplomacy, 34, 96
  and the press, 63–4, 114–15
  serious illness of, 18, 185, 192–3
  and Stalin, 15, 142–3, 156, 168–9, 170, 171–2, 176–8
Roosevelt, jun., Franklin, 59, 68, 111, 159
Roosevelt, Theodore, 15, 19
Rosenman, Judge Samuel, 212
Rutherford, Lucy Mercer, 19–23, 188
Rutherford, Winthrop, 19

Saint Lawrence River, 144
San Francisco Conference, 21
Sandhurst, 28
Saps at Sea, 79
Scharnhorst, 85
Sévigné, Madame de, 75
Sforza, Count, 203
Shakespeare, William, 144, 152
Shangri-La, 106, 131, 134
Sherwood, Robert E., 122, 137, 166, 179
Shoumatoff, Elizabeth, 20–3
Sinatra, Frank, 199

Index

Singapore, 86, 93
Smith, General Bedell, 134
Soames, Mary, 122
South Africa, 28
Spanish Civil War, 105
Spring, Howard, 52–3, 62
Stalin, Joseph, 15, 48, 56, 71, 101, 102, 103, 106, 141, 143, 156–7, 165, 168, 170–7, 200, 201, 204, 209, 211
Stalingrad, 175
Stark, Admiral Harold, 129
Stettinius, Edward R., 203
Stilwell, General Joe, 80, 130, 146, 157, 164
Suckley, Margaret, 21
Suez Canal, 167
Symbol, 108

Teheran, 156, 157, 165, 174–8
Time, 207
Torbruk, 88, 93, 213
Torch, 80, 92, 93, 104, 106, 107, 119, 141, 143
Trident, 129, 130, 137, 148
Truman, Harry S., 188
Tube Alloys, 89, 126, 136, 147
Tuscaloosa, USS, 58
Twain, Mark, 207

Unconditional Surrender, 114
United Nations, 21, 81

Versailles, Treaty of, 114
Vichy, 40, 48, 70, 104, 112, 114
Voroshilov, Marshal, 173

Wall Street, 24, 30
Wallace, Henry, 140
Warm Springs, Georgia, 18–19, 20, 25, 213
Watson, General 'Pa', 134, 164
Weimar, 23
Welles, Orson, 199
Welles, Sumner, 60, 61, 65
Wells, H.G., 29–30
Wharton, Edith, 19, 20
Whittier, John Greenleaf, 131, 133
Wilkie, Wendell, 41, 42, 44, 105, 108
Williamsburg, 130
Wilson, 197
Wilson, Theodore A., 73
Wilson, Woodrow, 18, 21, 24, 27, 29, 197
Winant, John Gilbert, 86
Wolfe, General, 144

Yalta, 203, 206, 207

Zanuck, Darryl F., 197